BROWN ASH BASKETS
A North American Tradition

by: Edmond, Joan & Brian Theriault

Master Tradition Basket Makers

Brown Ash Baskets

A North American Tradition

By; Edmond & Joan Theriault
& Brian J. Theriault

Theriault's Snowshoes

Fort Kent Maine U.S.A.

First published January 2020 (MMXX)

© Copyright Theriault's Snowshoes, Brian J. Theriault

Movie, DVD: Brown Ash Baskets: A North American Tradition,
Hard cover: Brown Ash Baskets: A North American Tradition,
  ISBN   9780991006977
Soft cover: Brown Ash Baskets: A North American Tradition,
  ISBN   9780991006915
eBook: Brown Ash Baskets: A North American Tradition,
  ISBN 9781645161509

All rights reserved. No part of this publication may be reproduced, distributed or transmitted in any form or by any means, without prior written permission.   Or stored in any electronic system, or transmitted in any form or by any means, electronic, mechanical, photocopy, recording, or otherwise, without written permission from the author, Brian J. Theriault.

Brian J. Theriault
P.O. Box 242
Fort Kent Mills, Maine 04744
U.S.A.

theriaultsnowshoes@gmail.com
Ilovesnowshoes.com
northamericasnowshoes.com

796.92
Crafts & Hobbies/general CRA 000000

Technical Assistance: Benjamin Latvis, Brian J. Theriault, Tracey Hartt, Garry Bouchard, John Bartlett, Louise Latvis, Matt Miller, Louise Bouchard, Corinne R. Douglass, Edmond Theriault, Joan Theriault
Design: Brian J. Theriault, Tracey Hartt, Louise Latvis
Cover Picture: Tracey Hartt
Family Picture: Jerry Jalbert
Photographs: Brian J. Theriault, Joan Theriault, Louise Latvis, Louise Bouchard, Joseph W. Davis

Aroostook County, Maine, U.S.A.

Printed in the United States of America

Brown Ash Baskets: A North American Tradition
By & Edmond & Joan Theriault & Brian J. Theriault
Master Basket Makers of over 50 years

<u>All AWARDS (Traditional Snowshoes)</u>

Brian J. Theriault

2020   Traditional Art Master Snowshoe Maker by the Maine Arts Commission, apprenticeship program. Apprenticeship is Matt Miller.

2019   Traditional Art Master Snowshoe Maker by the Maine Arts Commission, apprenticeship program. Apprenticeship is Benjamin Latvis

2017   Traditional Art Master Snowshoe Maker by the Maine Arts Commission, apprenticeship program. Apprenticeship is Hudson Labbe

2017   Maine Arts Commission's Award, Project Grant for Artists program, 2017 World Snowshoe Championships at Saranac Lake NY, Adirondacks USA

2015   Traditional Art Master Snowshoe Maker, Traditional Art Fellowship award by the Maine Arts Commission

2014   Artist Project Grant recipients, Maine Arts Commission, the making of traditional snowshoe and offering demonstration of the process during the 2014 World Acadian Congress

2013   Traditional Art Master Snowshoe Maker by the Maine Arts Commission, apprenticeship program. Apprenticeship is Jordan Labbe

2011   Traditional Art Master Snowshoe Maker by the Maine Arts Commission, apprenticeship program. Apprenticeship is Glenn Labbe

2005   Traditional Art Master Snowshoe Maker by the Maine Arts Commission, apprenticeship program.

Edmond Theriault

2017   Traditional Art Master Snowshoe Maker, **Traditional Art Fellowship award by the Maine Arts Commission**

Dedication

Henriette Blier (Pelletier) & Damase Pelletier

Isabelle Saucier (Pelletier) & Joseph Williams Pelletier

Joseph A. Theriault &
Effie Eva Babin (Theriault)

INTRODUCTION

The tree that has benefited our ancestors until today is the Brown (black) ash. It has furnished the raw materials for making sturdy light weight containers of all types and the fact that even if it gets wet, you can still use it. It is not known how many times you can get the containers wet and then dry them again; they seem to last forever. In the hands of experts, baskets of great beauty can be made with the materials.

A log from a good tree can make a lot of baskets. Look for a good growing ash tree that strips can bend without breaking. Knowing as much as you can about picking the tree will help you have fewer problems selecting the tree. We have worked with brown ash, which is sometimes called black ash in our area. Working with ash wood has given me a great opportunity to learn.

Be careful because there are other varieties of ash trees which will not work for baskets at all. Only brown ash works; only brown ash is useful for making baskets. Feeling the wood in your hands is a great pleasure. As you work the wood, you will have an easier time making baskets and become faster at completing the finished product. Learning even the littlest thing on basket making is always good. Even keeping notes can help you later.

Molds and patterns are great when starting out. Later, molds may not be needed as a weaver gains skills. Weavers learned how to control the shape and all other aspects of the basket. Achieving the feeling of completion and pride in the finished product is the end goal. These works of art will always have a place in our lives.

Be careful with the axe and the other tools that you will be using in making ash baskets. When it is swung upwards and hits a light, it came back on you. It's always good to do things at the same place where you know where everything is. People may try to help you and may move things around without you realizing it. Watch for the cloth's lines, pipes, or wires. Always check your work area first.

Processing tools are dangerous to use if you don't pay attention. If you have not worked with certain types of tool before, be extra careful. Use safe equipment such as safety goggles, gloves, or aprons where needed. Keep in mind what's around you. Many people forget objects that are around them or darkness may prevent you from seeing something. Watch for the person who is trying to help you. Know where they area and how close they are to you. Many things can go wrong, so keep everything in mind.

My father and I have been using brown ash for over fifty years to make traditional snowshoes. We use black ash because, once dried, it makes for a very light and strong snowshoe. Brown ash is also highly prized for making furniture because of the beautiful grain of the wood. Lumber can be made with trees that are not suitable for baskets. We have made kitchen cabinets and other products out of ash. We have made door frames once the ash was well dried and used ash plywood for the doors.

Edmond Theriault

Baseball bats made from ash are special. Reading the bat grain makes bats that will help the baseball player hit the ball further. Certain parts of the tree and the way it grows make a difference. Someday I'd like to make a bat to see if my knowledge of wood, the best growth rings, and a well growing tree can help create an exceptional bat. I know white ash is used more, is very important for items that need some flexibility.

THE FAMOUS POTATO PICKER: BY EDMOND THERIAULT

Prior to the arrival of the potato harvesters, all the potatoes in northern Maine were picked in brown ash baskets. The basket is round with an inverted 'u' shaped strong ash handle. It is very pliable to prevent bruising the potatoes and can be made different sizes. Potatoes must be dumped fast and carefully into cedar barrels to be transported to market or storage.

Pickers were instructed to lower the barrel side with one hand and dump the first basket all at once on the inner side as we lifted the barrel upright to prevent bruising. Most pickers preferred a basket that required four for a barrel so you could fill it in two trips as you went by the barrel. When the ground was damp and the baskets were wet, the dirt would stick to the basket making it heavier. You could take the basket by the rim and hit the bottom of the basket against the barrel to remove the caked dirt. Only an ash basket could take that kind of pounding and last almost forever.

It was about the time of the great depression that farmers were digging their potatoes with hand diggers. Then came the mechanical digger which was pulled by horses. That was about the time I started picking for my grandfather on his farm. I considered the

Edmond Theriault (96 years old) 2019

harvest a long picnic and never even thought of being paid. When I was about 13, some of the small farmers were hiring for one dollar a day from sunup to sundown. The farmer would tell you when he would start, and he would let you know. The farmer would say, "If you are good, I'll keep you."

My dad, who was a good picker, would go where there were large potato growers who would pay by the barrel plus board. At that time pickers had to load their barrel onto wagons with the help of the driver who was hauling the potatoes to storage. Barrels full of potatoes weigh about two hundred pounds if the barrel is not wet. The first time I picked with my brother, we were paid four cents per barrel. The two of us averaged close to two dollars each per day. We were paid less because we could not help loading our barrels of potatoes.

About this time a new digging machine with a gas engine was used. It turned a digger that dug two rows of potatoes at the same time so a picker could pick the two rows at the same time. The digger was still pulled by horses. The ash baskets and the hands of thousands of pickers were needed to gather the potato crop.

After I came back from World War II service and started raising a family, I would bring my children to learn how to use the ash basket. Some pickers dragged the basket; some lifted them

from place to place. Some pickers picked on their knees and rolled their baskets. I preferred just bending and rolling the basket with one hand until his basket got too heavy. Then I used both hands to roll it. By staying on my feet, I did not waste time getting up.

The horse was eventually replaced by tractors. It was not long after that the harvester came. That almost made the potato basket obsolete. These baskets trained many youngsters not to fear hard work. The new machines were so expensive that the small farmers could not make it. I wonder if my brother and I, who could each pick over a hundred barrels a day at twenty-two cents a barrel with just the use of an ash basket, was not a better deal. The most we ever picked between the two of us was 142 and 139 at 20 cent a barrel and board.

Tickets on barrels all had their own numbers, potato truck and grabbers were used at the time to move the barrels.

PREFACE

Making a traditional basket is not difficult, but it requires time. The effort you put in will allow you to take pride in the construction of a well woven basket that will last a long time. It took over fifty years to learn and acquire this knowledge. My father and I explain how to get the materials ready and steps to take to make baskets. We have made a lot of our own tools and developed our own tech niques to work the right wood. We learned through many trials. I would say that getting all the materials ready is the biggest step when preparing to make baskets.

The main theme of this book is to show you how you can make a pounded brown ash basket. This book will reveal the process from the standing tree to a completed basket. I document those steps, which will help you know how to create your own basket. I want to keep the art of traditional brown ash basket making alive, to share my knowledge and skills. There are other basket makers who have developed their own techniques. I hope by showing you my parents and my techniques for mak-

ing baskets, it can be done more easily and, in less time, while keeping the craftsmanship of the finished artwork. I want to show you the steps: procuring the tools, obtaining and processing the wood, weaving the strips, and finishing the rim.

With a few limited tools, baskets can be easily made. In this book, I will show how we fashioned our tools. We usually had to invent our own tools because these gadgets cannot be bought. We enjoy being creative and showing our talents, pursuing traditional ways discovered years ago. We use what we have around the shop to develop the tools, thinking though what the tools need to do. We create our tools to make our work easier and this allows us to make better baskets. We also bought a few tools that are too difficult to make getting the entire tools together make the next steps smoother.

Making brown ash baskets is a combination of amazing tasks. The first and most valuable task is getting strips of quality wood that are workable. If you can achieve this objective, the actual construction of the piece becomes an easier undertaking. It is often difficult finding good wood. Using excellent wood will make a very big difference. You will create a beautiful basket that is rugged and will last a long time.

Some of the same initial processes for preparing wood for traditional snowshoes are similar to basket making. We describe how we process and prepare the wood with the tools we invented, with our own spin. There are even fewer people who know to select the best brown ash trees for basket weaving. Remember you don't want to cut the grain of the wood any more than is needed because the grain is what will give the basket strength. Scraping the outside of the thicker pounded strip is also a must. This part is done right off because it works best when it is green and fresh. Then the strips are ready when you need them for usage.

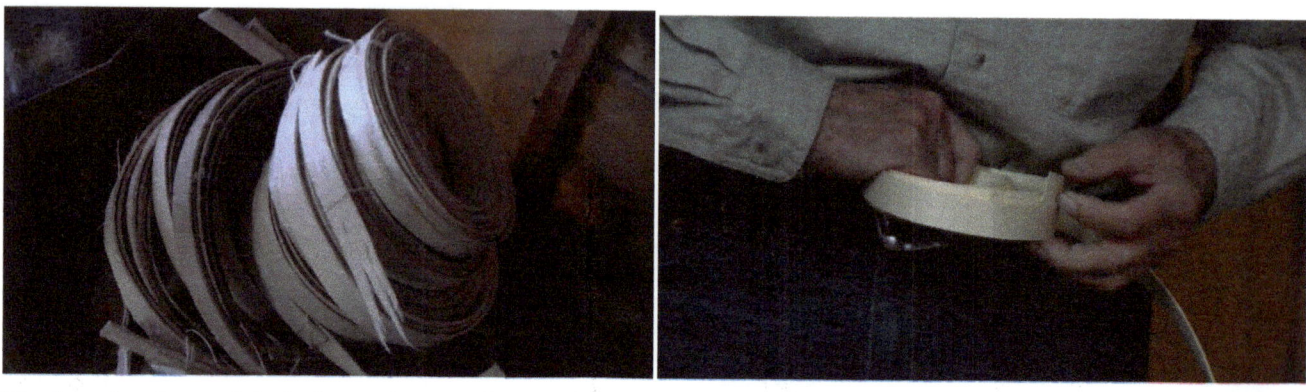

If ash strips have dried, the strips can be put into a container of warm water to soften. I like using cold water and keep check on the strips not to over soak them. If you do let them soak for a long time, the color will change and will not work as well because the water content in the wood is too high. Over soaked wood will shrink more once dry, making a basket with lots of spaces. This will not look very good, the weaver (the inlayed strip) could even move up and down making it a basket that could fall apart. If you want dark baskets by using a large glass jar of clear water with a lid works best to store strips for long periods of time, changes it to a deep brown color. You want to change the cold water every so often for best results.

Dyeing the strips is also best done in sealed jars to keep the air out. The dyeing colors can come from all kind of natural ingredients like blue berries and strawberries. It all depends on what color you may want. Basket making is a very old tradition which has been passed down through generations, keeping secrets within the family for how to make tools and styles for weaving. The most difficult thing to do is to prepare all the materials before starting to weave the basket. You need to think through the important steps to plan your basket. Before you start to weave, you need to have the shape/mold in mind, the weaving process, and finally the finishing steps to take to make a great basket.

If there is a way you can have all the prepared materials handy when you start to weave, it will reduce the time needed to finish your basket. The split strips with the extra smooth surface should be kept for the outside of the fancy baskets. They will look extra beautiful and will worth the most. Setting up the up rights in a clear pattern helps to hold your pattern. Another key element is to keep more tightening. Smaller spaces between strips will make for a tight basket.

Another skill that overlaps with snowshoe making is lashing the frame (rims) with rawhide. Using ash wood on the frame of the basket does not always make a smooth finish. Shoe leather nails

that have long sharp long points and that can be bent back in on the wood were used in the past. Nails didn't make a better, more durable, or an even more attractive basket. After basket usage, the nails would protrude on the inside the basket and many times, would injure your hands or the item being carried in the basket.

    Some weavers would wrap the rim by weaving strips of ash that are thinner and flexible to reinforce the rim of the basket. There is no need to steam the strips if the strips bend well. In basket making, the weaver usually finished the basket with their mark or end weave as a signature of their work. Some weavers even added a hidden strip so they could know that they were the creator of the basket. Others sign their work.

Just looking at a basket can often tell a story of how it was made and why. You don't always know who makes the basket but if they did a good job, you know it was a skilled basket maker and that the basket is going to last. Over many years, my father, Mother and I have developed our own techniques, with a little of a twist. You do not have to struggle gaining the skills we have learned throughout the years. The knowledge is there for you to make great baskets.

Care and patience are what makes a basket a work of art. One of the best things about basket weaving is that you will have a beautiful basket which can be passed down to your decedents; they can retain a great heirloom. Basket making can really be enjoyable, so just have fun. Do a nice job, and make a tight basket. Patienace will come to you after time. I think that this book will help you better understand how to get the materials and make a quality ash basket you will be proud of.

*****

The Abby Museum in Bar Harbor, Maine has a great collection of baskets and one time was a trading post on the shore of Frenchman Bay. I was in Cherry field, Maine one day and saw an old basket with a cover. I started telling things about the basket by looking at it. The gentleman in charge was really amazed about all I knew about the basket. I knew something about the maker but did not know who he was. All basket makers do things in certain way. If you had another basket of a maker, I can usually identify the same maker by the other basket he made.

You can learn a lot by how basket makers do things. You can see the materials they use, how they split the layers, and how they start the basket. You can see how they start at the bottom and weave the sides, and you can see how they finish the basket. The materials and placements of materials in the construction all tell a story. This basket I was looking at had a cover, which made me think of a laundry basket or a basket that had a cover to protect whatever was in it.

Joan Theriault

Table of Contents

Dedication --- 6
Introduction --- 7
The Famous Potato Basket Picker --- 8
Preface --- 10
Table of Contents --- 16
Magical Wood --- 19
Chapter 1 - My Early Life --- 22
Red Wooden Dog Sled --- 26
Chapter 2 - History of Basket Making --- 31
    Personal History of Basket Making --- 32
    Basket cconstruction --- 34
  Basket Makers --- 36
  Basket Collectors --- 37
Chapter 3 - Basket Types --- 40
    Rough Baskets/Potato Baskets --- 41
    Square Baskets --- 41
    Pack Baskets/Fishing Baskets --- 42
    Fancy Baskets --- 45
    Native American Baskets --- 47
    Interesting Facts --- 50
Chapter 4 - Basket Planning --- 55
    Hand Tools --- 58
    Homemade Tools --- 61
    Electric Tools --- 70
    Other Equipment --- 71
Chapter 5 - Trees (brown ash/black ash/swamp ash) --- 79
    Ash Tree Types --- 80
    Selecting the Tree --- 81
    Testing the Wood --- 83

Storing the Tree---89

Harmful Insects---90

Chapter 6 - Wood working--92

Log Method---95

Stick Method---100

    Steps for Making Strips--101

    Cutting Sticks---101

    Pounding Sticks---105

Spitting Strips---106

Scraping--108

Storing Strips---111

Dyeing, Colors---114

Special-Dyeing: By Joan Theriault--116

Chapter 7- Rawhide--137

Getting a Cow Skin---137

Storing a Cow Skin---139

Processing Skin - Needed Equipment--139

Set-Up--140

Processing the Hide--140

Removing Hair---142

Fleshing the Hide on the Beam---142

Stretching--145

Cutting--146

Caring for Rawhide--148

Tips--149

Chapter 8 -Basket weaving---160

Preparing with a Plan---160

Basket Mold Frames--161

Molds---162

    Free Hand Mold---162

    Frame Mold---162

    Take Down Mold--162

    Pack basket Mold--163

Preparing to Weave--168

Weaving---172
        Single Layer Weave---172
        Wrap Around Weave--172
        Chase Weave--172
    Bottom---174
    Finishing Top Weave---178
    Bending Around the Rim--178
    Nails---182
    Handle--184
    Nails on Handle--190
    Wrapping---190
Chapter 9- Basket Making---200
Chapter 10 - Care of basket--219
Chapter 11 - Continuing knowledge---221
Chapter 12 – Pictures--228
Conclusion---231

Magical Wood

(Brown Ash Basket)

By Brian J. Theriault

Stump to finished usable baskets.

The process takes time and hard work.

Many years of well-kept secrets are now in your hands.

Traditions of an old art are part of our heritage.

Work with your hands to create a gift for life.

Caring stuff in a brown ash basket is a way that we can remember from the past.

Stump to finished usable baskets.

The process takes time and hard work.

Many years of well-kept secrets are now in your hands.

We didn't have much money, but we had the time to learn.

We were willing to work hard.

We loved working with ash wood.

Stump to finished usable baskets.

The process takes time and hard work.

Many years of well-kept secrets are now in your hands.

As years went by, we then become basket makers.

As a family we worked together, making it fun and enjoyable.

As time went by, we made all kinds of different baskets we used.

Stump to finished usable baskets.

The process takes time and hard work.

Many years of well-kept secrets are now in your hands.

To keep this alive we wrote a book with many pictures.

To keep this alive we did a DVD on how-to.

To keep this alive, you need to buy a book and DVD.

Stump to finished usable baskets.

The process takes time and hard work.

Many years of well-kept secrets are now in your hands.

Brian J. Theriault

• CHAPTER 1 •

MY EARLY LIFE

My older brother wanted to make an ash pack basket to use while in the great Maine outdoors. One day, my father, brothers, and I got a brown ash tree from the nearby woods. We put the log into the basement, where we lived in Fort Kent, Maine. We started pounding directly on the green tree with the back side of an axe. I remember my father and other bothers hitting that brown ash log all day long, each taking turns.

The ceiling of the cellar was low, so you had to be careful not to hit the metal ducts or the house beams. We let the axe fall and bounce on the horizontal six-foot log. We could smell the furnace working as we kept hitting the trunk with the back of a three-foot axe. We turned the log, trying to hit each section to loosen the wood fiber layers. Dust would lift around the room as the axe came down with a thud. Each time we lifted the axe our muscles would pull upward. We each worked for about ten minutes before our shoulders got sore. We took turns, continually pounding for as long as we could. We were not going to let the ash log win, even though our arms were ready to fall off.

We anxiously waited until each layer loosened. We pulled one or more layers at a time, cautiously trying to get larger continual pieces of the layer. We pounded some more, lifting several layers one-by-one until we were close to the inside three-inch diameter. The process was very tiring, but once we had the strips, we were ready to try putting them together to make a basket.

I do not believe my brother had a mold when he made the first pack basket, and the internet was not available to goggle what other people had tried. A mold would have supported the shape. We wove the pieces together, learning the ins and outs of making a tight basket. With the weaver pieces sticking up, we had to figure out how to finish off the basket, nails being used at that time. This was over forty-five years ago, a time when we were young and had the energy and will power to conquer his project the hard way.

*****

This big pack basket is one of the first basket ever made by the Theriault's.

My father used potato baskets all his life, picking up to 142 barrels of potato in one day when he was much younger. At that time, pickers would get 20 cents a barrel. The barrel weighed about one hundred eighty to two hundred pounds when it was full. It took four good size baskets full of potatoes to fill a barrel. Working hard and long days never bothered him. I had big steps to follow being his son. Picking potatoes is not one of the tasks I could match him.

I remember using a potato basket when I was very young. For many years, I used pounded ash baskets for picking potatoes on the fields. Brown ash baskets were dipped in an acid bath to prevent against bacterial wilt and any other diseases in 1940. When I worked in the seventy's in a potato house, we had to step into a pan with boots in special disinfectant.

I know firsthand how durable and long lasting a basket can be. They can endure many years,

withstanding muddy elements. The crusted muddy baskets lasted through being hit on the side of a potato barrel many times to loosen the dirt. Those baskets were left lying upside down next to the barrel to keep it out of the weather at night. I had respect for these baskets and relied on the people who would make them.

We didn't have the money to buy baskets, and we had the time, so we got there and made baskets. We did buy some tools we needed, but mostly we made our own tools. We also made our molds and other things to make baskets. Starting at a young age was very helpful because it was easier to learn. Practice and good habits made the task faster and easier.

Basket making was a family hobby because most of my family worked with their hands. We all participated in this endeavor. We used pack baskets and other baskets throughout our lives. I've seen my family use basket in many other ways, at times sell a few or give a few, but we kept many of them. We used pack baskets, decorative baskets, fishing baskets, and storage baskets. We saw their usefulness and wanted to make them.

*****

Red Wooden Dog Sled

My mother's father owned a red wooden sled, which was pulled by a big black dog they owned. This sled could be used to pull all kinds of things that fit, such as two water barrels. It could be used for so much more. I had not really known this information until about three years ago. It is amazing the information you may hear when you listen to older people talk about the past. We actually used this sled for bringing logs out of the woods to make baskets and snowshoes. It worked very well and still can be used today. This is a part of the history and heritage that goes very far back. We don't even remember who made the sled.

*****

My family sure learned a lot by trial and error. My mother, Joan, is a talented fancy basket weaver. She can control the twists and shape as she works out the pattern. My father, Edmond, and I prefer processing the wood into the strips and sizing the weavers to the correct widths needed for the baskets. We do make pack baskets, and other types of baskets, but are better known for making traditional snowshoes. It was a natural progression since the materials used are so closely related; both use brown ash.

Working with my hands feels good to me. Over the years, as my hands have developed calluses, the feel of the wood between my fingers takes me back in time. I went into snowshoe making after years of working with wood. I wrote a book with my father, *Leaving Tracks: A Maine Tradition*. This is a how-to book explaining the steps and giving details to make Theriault's traditional snowshoes. We regard this usable art form as high quality traditional snowshoes.

We make traditional snowshoes out of the same kind of brown ash trees as pack baskets. The relationship between baskets and snowshoe making includes using some of the same skills. Looking back, I'm glad that things happened as they did. I know it has played a big role in my life. Working as a family and working with my hands was fun. This great hobby bonded our family, especially when the family got a chance to take the first steps onto a smooth white blanket of snow. I'm pretty sure my ancestors in the North American had many skills to survive in this harsh climate, and this tenacity somehow was instilled in me.

*****

The elders are a great source of support and knowledge. We did have a few basket makers around, which was helpful. You could ask some questions, but you still needed to work at it yourself to really appreciate it. Once a way of life has now become more of a traditional art form.

Our father and mother, Edmond & Joan Theriault: oldest to youngest: Alvin, Wanda, Brian, Galen, Anne, Louise, Marian, Lila, Aileen, Laurie, and Edmond Jr. (Eddie). Family pictures by Jerry Jalbert on this page.

Notes:

Madison Theriault

• CHAPTER 2 •

HISTORY OF BASKET MAKING

    The Baskets have been utilized and manufactured around the world for many generations. The materials to create these containers depended mostly on the materials in the environment. The shape and construction depended on the needs of the people using them. Baskets have a great history that has evolved into the skilled craft today. Every basket tells a story. In the past, making ash baskets was well known because many people produced and used them makers past them on to others. The brown ash pounded baskets were made by hand. The baskets were often light weight and strong. They could be used for so many purposes. The bonus was that they lasted a long time at a low cost.

With just an axe, a man could go in the woods and cut an ash tree of the needed length. He could then start pounding on the whole length of that piece of tree with the head of the axe. The growth rings would loosen where the tree was pounded. Starting from the top of the piece, he could start a certain width strip and pull it off the tree. This history and tradition need to be kept alive; it's our heritage. This is a very special skill that few people know and can develop into a finished product. It's been a big part of our past and needs to be kept alive for the future. I can never say it enough.

PERSONAL HISTORY OF BASKET MAKING

My family started making baskets over fifty years ago. We started with getting a tree and pounding on it. Being from a big family and making what we needed was a way of life. I remember hitting that tree log with the back of axe most of that day. We decided to make baskets, not knowing how hard or time consuming the process was. We saw people with baskets but did not recognize or appreciate the work behind the task at that time. This, however, did not stop us because we never looked at tasks like this as hard work.

Our family worked together in the ash basket process at one time or another. We looked around and used what we had to make things. Our creative mind, working together, was a big plus. Once we determined what we wanted to do, all we need to do was put our bodies to work. We had a can-do-attitude, no matter how much time was needed. The hard work never scared us.

For myself, I really enjoy making things with my hands and using my mind to be creative to build my own path. I learned a lot from working with my parents. We all came up with our own tools and techniques to make baskets, and it was okay to change things a bit when a better way was discovered

I did go see a few basket makers with my dad, but we often found that their way had not progressed. It may have worked for them, but not for us. We were often creative in our ideas and did it our way; we liked blazing our own trails. Be it hunting, fisherman, all around outdoors men, we developed our knowledge to find a better way. We had to also remember that we had the time, but not necessarily the money. I always had a good time doing anything outdoors.

When I go demonstrating, many people come and tell me stories. They want to share their knowledge. They look to be a part of the knowledge wheel that is always turning and expanding. After making baskets for years and people wanting to learn how to make their own or buy them, we started teaching pack basket making. There was a high demand for constructing your own pack basket. When they get to work on hands-on learning basket making skills, they have reached the hub of the wheel where they are not only learning the process but experiencing fulfillment of accomplishing a task. The hands-on learning helps solidify the knowledge.

I got thinking how much I know about baskets and basket making, which includes working with ash wood most of my life. I have learned so much and know what I'm looking at. That is one reason I'm writing this book, to give knowledge to others. It is a tradition we don't want to lose. The old ways and the easier newer ways sometimes need to be meshed together to create the basket that people want. Getting away from the tradition can be good, while also keeping the past adds to the creation. At times, it is the money that makes basket makers go to the more modern look and style. Ultimately, we want to also keep some parts of the past.

BASKET CONSTRUCTION

Basket making is an art form that has been passed down from a long time ago, and there is a lot of skill and hard work that goes into basket making. Many hand tools can be made with the things that are around. It's unreal how people come up with these creative ways of doing things. The method with weavers, woven under the basket, while bent over at the corner with ends bent in is ingenious. The weaving with fine weavers makes a basket so much stronger. It has a beautiful appearance. The designs within the weaving show the great skill of the weaver. When you make baskets that you are proud of, they will be sought after by the many collectors. One does not need to be rich to make baskets.

I found a very old basket, which I have added to my collection. It is nice to examine how the basket was made at that time. The way the handle is made, bent in at the end, and wrapped with an

ash strip covering over the handle is different from the wood strip and nail finish. The loop of the bent strip was used to make a round loop to hold the handle in place. This was a great way to keep the handle secure while keeping the basket very strong and attractive. It would be interesting to know who the weaver was, when it was made, and how long it took to make the baskets.

      It is important to use the better materials for the upright strips and weavers for baskets. Good quality wood should be used to make sturdy hand potato baskets, as this is the best tool for moving potato. Baskets can take a pounding and take the outdoor weather during its lifetime, which are many years if you take care of it. Shaped molds and good handles are a must in basket making. With the year's growth going the same way, the outside of the handle will look stylish.

      The basket becomes your hand-crafted creation. You will also have a basket which is not only sturdy but will outlast most store-bought baskets available. You will take pride after taking a tree and processing it to make something useful and beautiful. It may be the hobby that you have been looking for.

BASKET MAKERS

In the past, many people knew how to make ash baskets. People made them and past them to others. Some of these techniques have been passed down for many generations, hundreds of years. In the past, all members of a family would be involved in the basket making process, no matter how old you were. In this way every member of a family would learn the various techniques at every stage. Baskets were used for so many things. They were light weight and strong. They lasted a long time.

There are many basket makers that make ash baskets, but very few that get or know how to get their own ash. Even, if they might know where and how to get wood, they tend to buy it instead. The best thing you can do is get your own tree and know the quality of the wood as you work it. Work the wood yourself so you know what you have.

You can tell a lot about the makers by examining a basket. You can check the wood or tree that they start with. You can see if the baskets are made using all the same growth rings or all the same splint ones. Taking more time to choose the wood and knowing how to work it into the finished product will create a great work of art. By looking at the weaving and materials, you can tell a lot about the maker. It is hard sometimes, to know who made the basket because basket makers were not always recognized.

The right wood quality and sizing thickness of the ash is very important to instill quality and strength. Well prepared wood strips make it easier to weave. The rim is another place you can tell how good a basket maker is. Is made in a rough or clunky manner? Can you get a splinter or scratch from an outlying nail? You can see the process for making different baskets allowing you to think about the quality.

Experience will bring excellence. Quality ash baskets will be in demand with a high price. Everything you do can make a difference so take your time and do quality work. Pay attention to those details that will make you stand out. Look at other baskets. This will help you visualize your own basket and it helps to develop your own ideas. It will help you to learn more. Sometimes you can just look at a basket and identify the maker. Quality of wood, workmanship and experience will bring you excellence. Your ash baskets will be in high demand.

Our elders are great source of knowledge, which can help our learning. It is very important to respect them and thank them for they are the teacher of the world. I have learned a lot from my elders and other basket makers, mostly by looking at their baskets. Understanding and patience are very important. Think of all the time it has taken for them to learn their knowable and then the time it takes to show others the correct steps to take.

Basket Collectors

Basket collectors are special people that have helped to keep basket making alive. They usually recognize the quality of the baskets and help keep a good basket maker busy. Baskets, for the most part, are to be used. They are often used for containers. They are great in pictures and for artistic home decor.

Usually collectors want a signed basket to know who the maker is. The name on the basket or the quality and the story behind the baskets is very important. It also depends on what the collector is looking for at that time. They want the basket in good condition. Museums pay for some basket they would like in their collections. We do have some basket makers today earning a money-making basket, which shows they have great skills. This book is also good for collectors because they will know what they are looking at and what questions to ask about the baskets.

Note:

• CHAPTER 3 •

BASKET TYPES

Baskets have elegance to their usefulness. There isn't any other container that can hold up to this product. It can take the cold or heat of weather conditions. Its material can take heavy use and is flexible. Even when it is continually hit, it can still hold on to its shape.

Styles of baskets often depend on the person making the basket and its intended use. When you consider your own basket, have an idea in mind as to the style of basket you would like to make before you start.

The more thought and skill you put into it, the more you will get out of it. Knowing your wood, making your tools, preparing the wood, and making good forms are excellent ways to prepare. Keeping notes is a great way to check your progress. Learning should always be a part of what you do, so evaluate your work.

ROUGH BASKETS/POTATO BASKETS

Some people do not cut every other upright piece or rims of baskets. Some bend them all with the finish of the inside and outside bend of the basket. Potato and pack baskets often have a coarse finish. The strength and sturdiness are the concern, rather than then quality and elegance. These baskets might be made quickly because of the rough use. Looks are not so important to the maker and user. I say do not use junk because it will make junky baskets, but for potato baskets, it might be used. Knots are okay in some places on potato baskets if the wood is strong. Potato basket needs to be tight and may take more time to complete as the wood dries and it continually tightened.

SQUARE BASKETS

Square baskets use thick wood ash strips, maybe ¼" thick straight pieces for uprights. A very thin outside bendable rim is what we do to make a nice square basket that is very useful. Thin round handles on the longer sides are easy to place on the outside of baskets. A nail on each side of the handle is all that is needed. A measurement of four inches high, thirteen inches long, and five inches wide is just one example of a size template that can be used. Once the process to make baskets is known, endless possibilities are available to make baskets that match your desirers.

PACK BASKET

We make a wide opening pack basket for carrying larger items. Pack baskets are used to carry all kinds of things. It was invented so you would not have to carry it in your hands. You can carry things on your back more easily. It is light weight and a great size to fit on your back. If you do outside actives, it is a must have.

Pack baskets need wooden cedar runners in order to keep off the ground and dry. Sometimes liners may be used to keep the basket dry inside. You may want to remove the liners at times to allow the wood to fully dry. Putting a lid on top is a good idea. It helps to keep your items protected from the elements. You can make the cover out of plywood.

FISHING BASKETS

Fishing creel made from ash are the best because it keeps the fish cool, and the wood can take many years of slimy fish. Thin strips are used to make a tight horizontal weave that still allows airflow. It is made with a flat side to fit along the side of your body, and the top is sloped away from you a bit to allow your arm to rest. Make it to fit on your side with a strap. A small hole in the top of the creel makes it easy to put a fish in, but also prevents the fish from coming out easily if you fall or bend over for something. You need to wash the basket after each use and let it dry right off. I even carry my drinks and food in my creel before I catch fish to place it there.

Fancy Baskets

     The best quality wood is used for fancy basket. This is the type of basket that shows the real skill with creative designs. The shape and designs on the outside of the basket is not obvious on the finished product. To make these perfect loops, you must use the same wood peg mold sizes to make all loops look alike. Glass, wood marbles, or just about anything you want can be used keep the shape. They should be all the same size and done when making the basket. They can even be left as part of the work.

Fancy basket strips can be added on with a tight twist on the outside of basket. It takes time to dry the twirls with pegs inside were wanted. Check every now and then to make sure they look and keep their shape as they dry. You still can adjust at this time when putting twirls on and or drying. They are dry when the pegs are loose. It works like a small mold or form you want to create for the loops on the basket.

Fancy basket rims are usually tied with thin ash weavers. If your fancy basket will be used a lot, it would be better to tie the rims with rawhide. Baskets can go beyond the rim for new fancy baskets and even could have two rims and even more rims for a fancy basket that you do not see often if at all. Some people make art basket that may not even be used to carry stuff in, but to look at and put on a shelf on a wall or wall art. Regarding shapes; baskets can be woven into fruits, vegetables, animals, shells, and many other objects of various sizes and colors.

Sometimes adding just a few color strips to your basket brings a nice look and creates uniqueness to your baskets. Some fancy small baskets may use only the white split strips. When making fancy small baskets, it is desirable to use the white sap wood (strips) that bend more easily and have a better appearance. Pick and choose carefully your matching strips for looks and thickness when making a fancy ash basket. This will give you the desired looks for which fancy baskets are known. Split strips of the same thickness can be put on the outside of a fancy ash basket.

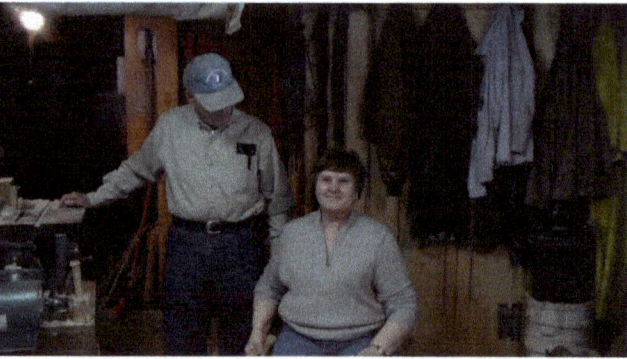

NATIVE AMERICAN BASKETS

Native American baskets are made with the high skill level of the artist. These are often worth more money. There are many usages, along with many sizes and shapes. Every basket was made for a reason, with quality being a number one concern. Trading baskets were very

well known in the history. Native Americans often used their tribal colors and designs on their baskets to identify groups in different geographical areas.

Decorations

Porcupine quills

Porcupine quills on an ash basket design put a good touch of class and traditionnel flare.

Shells can also be add

Sea Grass or sweet grass

Cattails and many other items

    Many baskets makers would, and still do, incorporate animal bone, fur, feathers, and other gifts from nature into their baskets, making them an artistic expression of their own creation. Incorporating elements like roots, split roots, birch bark strips, sweet grass, braided rope, yarn or any other natural highlights will really make your baskets unique. Also, rawhide, bones and rocks are great examples that can make a basket really come alive. Non-permanent items such as flowers, and other seasonal feathers you can create these add on so that they simply snap on or off.

    Some makers go further and make art out ash strips as part of the art. Baskets can be made with many types of barks, drilled holes, and ash weaved together tying them together. But this just shows you that you will see all kinds of things that you can incorporate into your baskets if you want the sky in the limit. We sometimes add a touch of own and put miniature snowshoes to put on the baskets. Try miniaturizing your interest to develop your own style and identity.

INTERESTING FACTS

A basket is a durable container made of the natural wood of trees.

The wood layers will come apart when pounded. It is the quality of the basket and its maker that make it art. It does take a skill to make expert baskets.

1. Brown ash wood is light weight once dry.
2. Brown ash is easy to pound. It gets the year wood rings to separate.
3. Brown ash is easy to use and spit.
4. The wood can be made into a strong container for many things.
5. The wood is easy to shape into baskets for it intended usage.
6. Brown ash is a light weight, soft wood, with a strong grain with lasting qualities. (It can take the outdoor weather very well.)
7. The wood strips are easy to store until needed. They can be rolled up and placed in paper bag.
8. Baskets are a useable art, which can fetch a high price. Quality baskets can sell very easily.
9. Basket making is an old art form that has been passed down through many generations.
10. The maker has control. We put our own spin on picking the right tree, developing tools and molds, using rawhide, and producing the basket our way.

~ 53 ~

Note:

• CHAPTER 4 •

Basket Planning

NOTE: Before investing in expensive equipment, try it by hand. You may get more out of the experience. Learning the traditional way is the best way if you desire a quality finished product.

Think about the different baskets you have seen and understand the possibilities of what you can make. A good plan and plenty of time can set you up for a great basket.

Start with all your tools and ash strips ready.

Place strips in a way to make the bottom of the basket.

Hold down and or pin down the bottom in place.

Start weaving in a clock wish direction with narrower strips, depending on the basket.

Keep moving the uprights straight as you move up the basket.

Place onto the mold currently if you are to use one.

Weave around three rows and then let dry for some time.

Use the 'doughnut hole plywood ring' with heavy weight on the bottom when not weaving. This keeps the basket bottom flat and shaped correctly.

As weaving, start tightening at the beginning first and retighten the weavers, then continue to weave three more rows.

Repeat from the beginning until you are at the top and stop.

Wait about 12 hours, and then retighten from the start for the last time.

Place the basket top, upside down in water in a container of water so you can bend the rib ends once soaked. Water level should be up to the bend and not the weavers that go around.

Go around the basket cutting the ends to desired lengths. Once the ends are cut and bent over inside will be seen.

Rims inside and outside are now put in place and clamped as you go around.

Handles, if needed, are connected at this time.

Handles are pre-made for the size of the baskets. Once you know the rim size, the notch is made just before it is put on. (The handle size fits the basket of inner rim of the basket).

Rims pieces are placed so they do not land together and are tapered so they are the same thickness.

Weave around the rim with ash weaver around currently.

Tuck the end and weave around with clamps, many needed as you go around counterclockwise.

If rawhide is used, then you must clamp and drill holes in center of uprights and go around the rim with knots.

Clamps are left on until the rim is dried. Clamping the overlap is very important to keep in place.

Trim lose wood hairs on the baskets if there is any and lightly sand the basket.

Signing the bottom of the basket or wherever is done at this time, or not to let people know who made it.

This is the time to put on a finish if you want or not.

Precise tools are very important. On whatever part you are working on, a sharp edge is needed to make specific cuts. Good files or stones are a must to keep your tools sharp. Use wet or oil stones to sharpen your tools. Sharp tools will also make thing easier when it comes to cutting the wide ash strips precisely. Cut strips one or a few at a time. When working with these tools for making baskets, care should be taken to work safely. Take the time to needed for every aspects of basket making and remember that sharp tools are a must because they will make your work easier.

A crooked knife is also used in designing baskets, creating snowshoes, and many other art forms where wood is used. It is not hard to make a crooked knife. It is handy to have one, with the bonus of reminding you of the old ways of the woodsman. Usually you make a custom crooked knife to fit your hand just right.

Scraping is best done on the strips that are about one inch wide. If strips are too wide, it will be harder to scrape. Place leather on the knee over your pants for safety. With your left hand, hold the knife on the strip. Leave the knife in place at a slight angle with pressure just enough to remove the wood ridges. With your right hand, pull slowly until you know the speed needed to do a proper job scraping. The knife should be sharp and kept with the sharp end flat to the strip at a 45-degree angle. A few times on each surface may be needed. Flip the strip to where you have a strong hold and pass the knife until the strip is cleaned.

Scraping is done by pulling the sharp edge towards you. We made a tool that is on a table. When standing, use both hands to scrape easily. Control the pressure with your left hand and pull with the right hand with the strip being pulled at a slight angle. Pull a bit at a time at a slight angle on the blade. Deepen the pressure and the speed when you pull. This will work the best. After some time, gaining the feel and the skill to go faster, the job will improve.

HAND TOOLS

One critical hand tool that can be easily made is the awl, a sharp nail with a handle. It will be used many times. You should keep it next to you. Having several different sizes would be great. The awl is used to make holes in wood, rawhide, and leather with a simple and quick push and turn. It can even help move the uprights and slide in the weavers. Two or three or more axes will be useful for the different jobs. Bottom left hand crank sizer for ash strip, bottom right, increment borer.

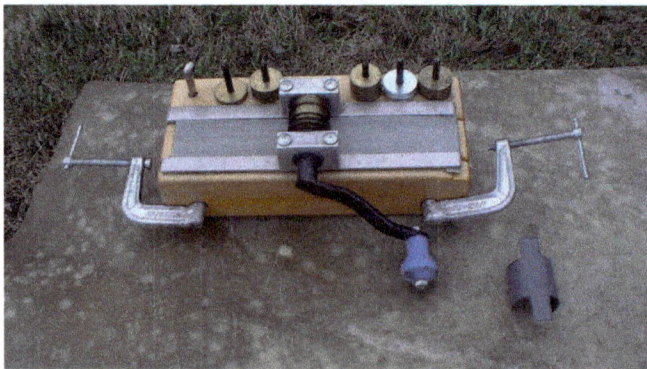
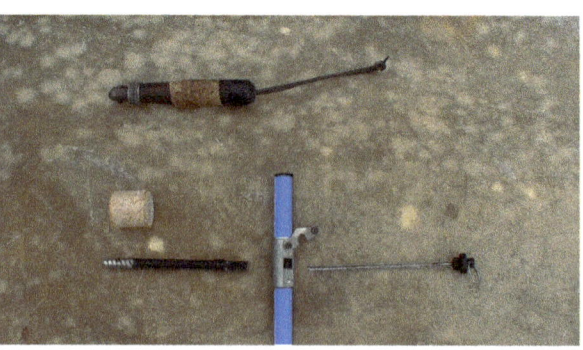

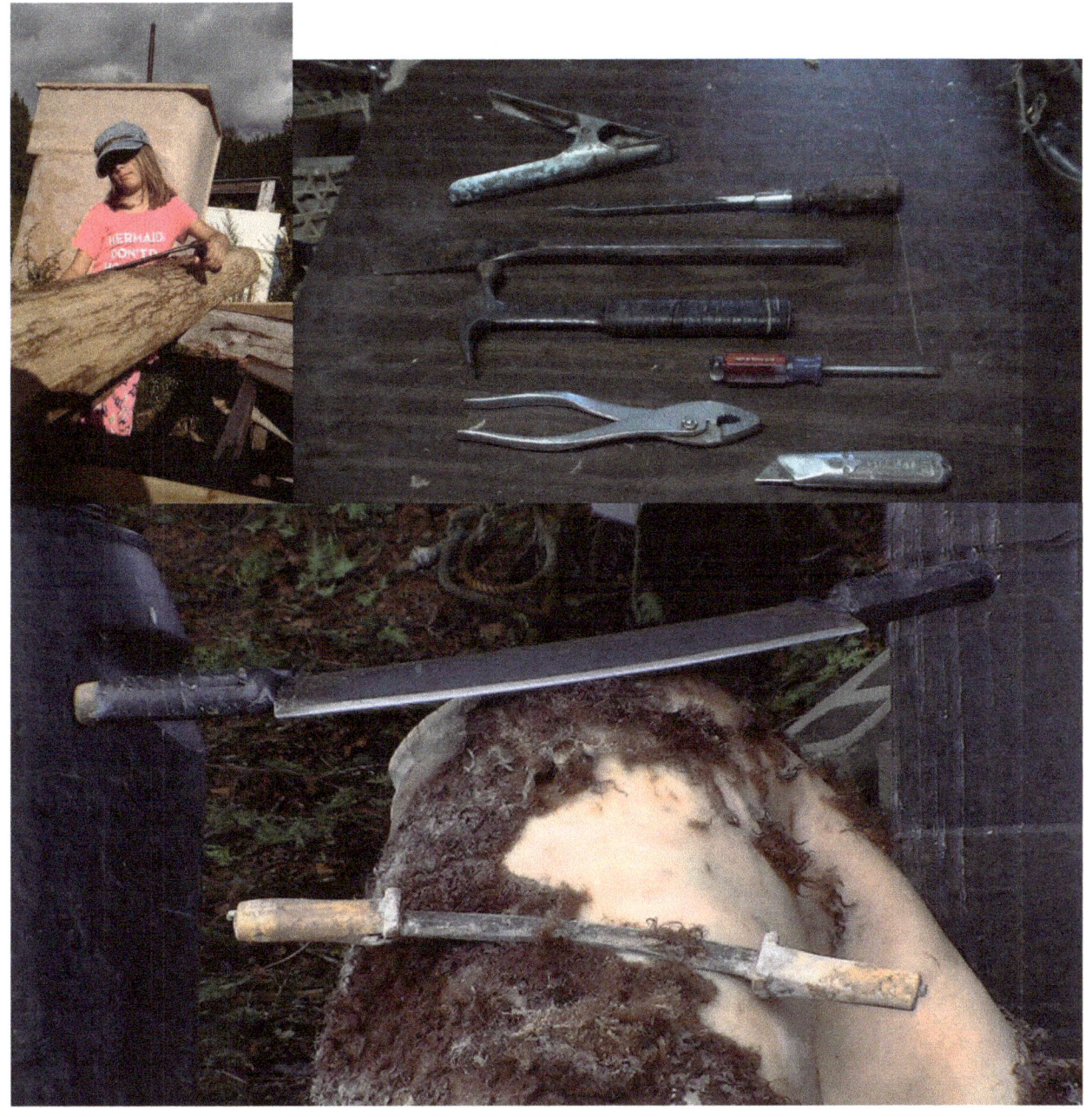

Top left, wood draw shaver, bottom picture, two handed big flesher, and smaller flesher and dull side hair remover.

Wood short work horses for the log to lay on and easy to work on.

Homemade Tools

Make a wooden wedge tool with a point about 9" long made from ash crosspiece. This control stick is used to move weaving strips down or sideways on the inside or outside of basket as you weave. It can be used to tighten the basket and can be made to different sizes as needed. Using the stick to move the basket ash strips closer together will make the weave tighter. Use the flat part for most of the moving but be careful because the ash can only take so much pressure. Go clockwise when tightening.

Top left, wood point ash strip mover. Top right, shaving horse.

Center left, crooked knife. Center right ash splitter.

Bottom are ash strip scrapper with ball bearings, next picture on top left is also the same tool.

Next page, top right is a handmade splitter with ball bearings. We have made a lot of own tools.

A common 5" spike, which has been flattened one-inch point and bent to a ninety-five-degree angle, one inch from the point, is a critical tool to work with the ash strips when weaving. A handle makes it easier to hold the spike. Flatten the point with a hammer and other end put handle on off first. Make a hole in a short dowel and glue the spike in the hole tight. Making different types and sizes, even with nails for the smaller ones would be great to work with. If you can get deer or moose sheds for handles, it would look even better. When the weave is tight, it will be only that tool that can be inserted under the weave to slide and tighten the basket. Always go in the same direction as you weave when tightening the basket pulling tight.

Old handheld type splitters had many small pointy blades sticking up. These are hard to use unless you are a skilled person that using it, which we don't have one. We have a homemade crank splitter with an angled blade. The splitter my father and I came out with had only one blade with a ball bearing to help with the splitting friction. We like to make tools that are more friendly and easier to do the work at hand. It works with one size width at a time. It works

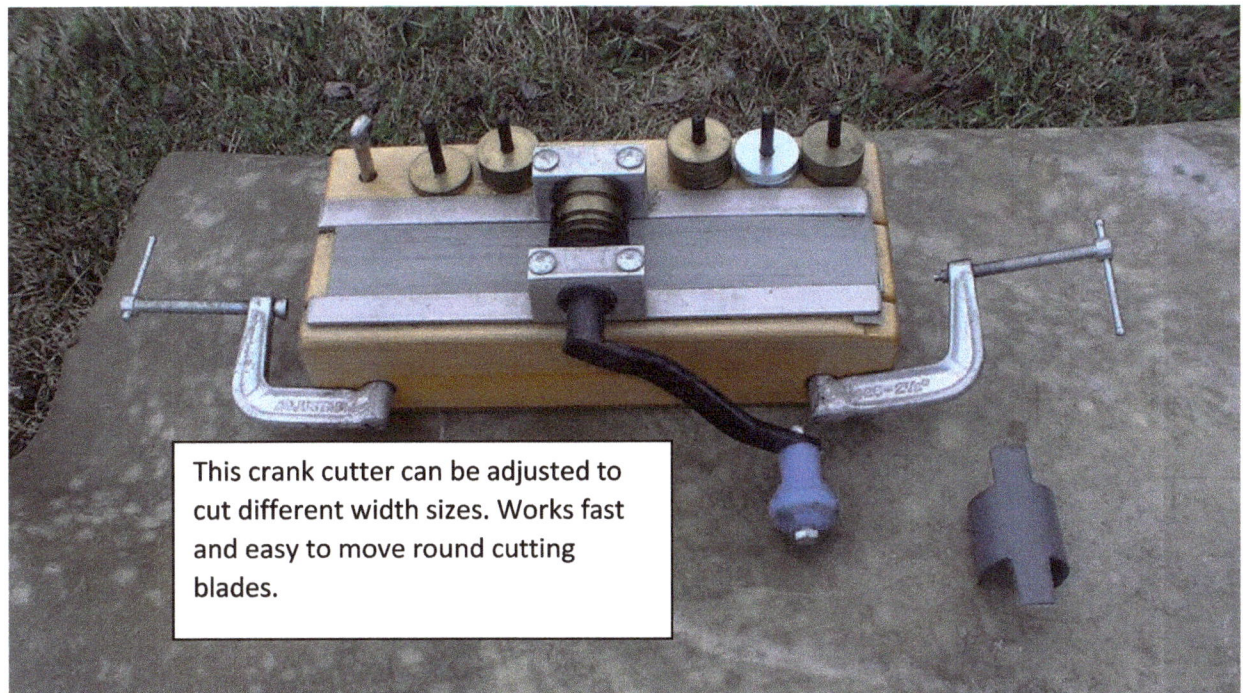

This crank cutter can be adjusted to cut different width sizes. Works fast and easy to move round cutting blades.

well and easy to use. This tool works best because you can control the splitting and even change the tension by flipping the layer to split another way. Ball bearing rollers gives more control, making it faster and easier. You can see exactly how it is splitting. It can be flipped around and a knife cut can help make it run back in place. One side moves and the other side doesn't.

My knowledge of wood and baskets give me a better understanding of the tools. The easier you make it for people to learn and work on the strips, the more enjoyable the activity will be for people who want to make their own baskets.

Learning how to use the different splitting tools is very important. Try different ways to get a better understanding of what works best for you. You may find your own easier or faster way depending on your skill level. Getting the best tree is one thing that will always be critical for best results. Keep to the tradition way as much as possible. Add your own spin to make it easier. After you have learned the more modern ways, you may want to learn and use the older tools. Sharp tools always work best when cutting wood. Safety is always very essential.

Hand made hard wood mallets, different sizes for different people and the way you want to pound.

Metal pipe in a stand to help the pointy nails go back into the inside of rim of the basket.

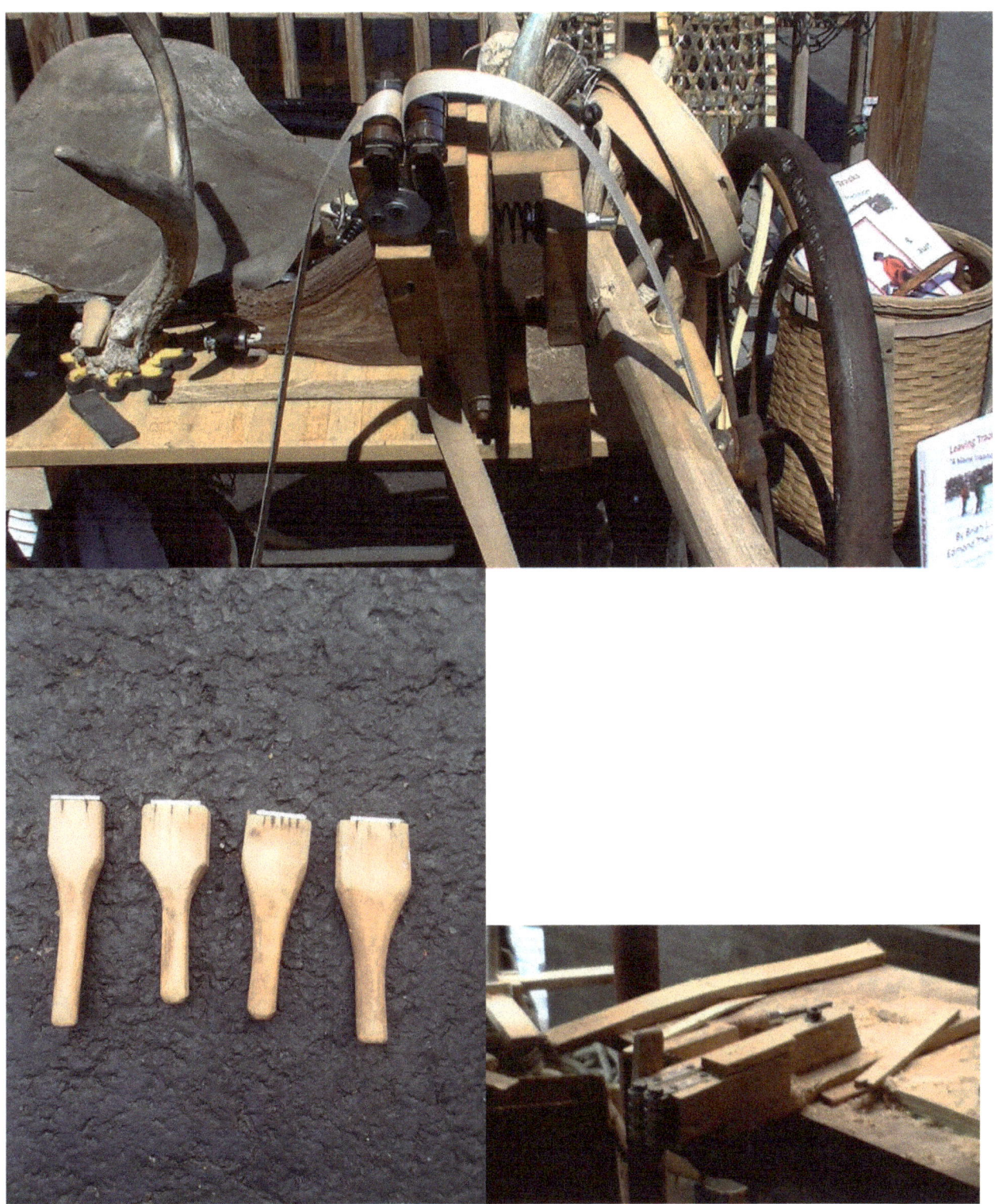

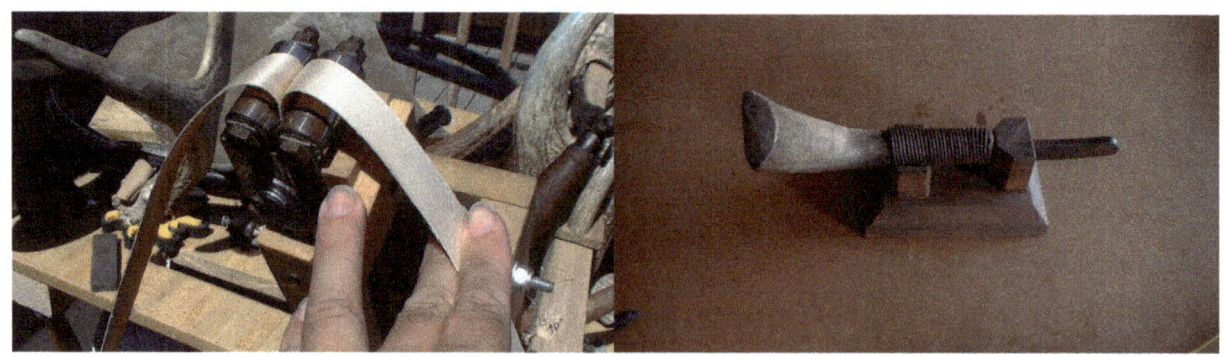

Electric Tools

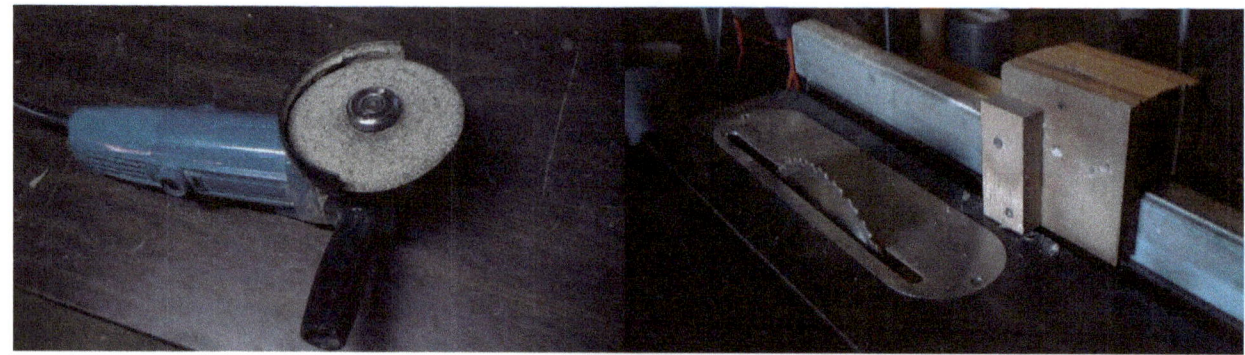

Sander

8" skill saw for stripping the log.

Keeping traditions alive.

10" Table saw, with a wooden block on the fence.

OTHER EQUIPMENT

Safety equipment should be used when cutting trees or even going into the woods.

Chainsaw

Keep this tool in great working condition. Learn how to use a chainsaw and fell a tree before heading out to get your tree.

EQUIPMENT TO AVOID

Big equipment, like feller bencher, can damage parts of the tree that you want to use. This may seem like the easier way to go, but you do not want to waste parts of the tree. A skidder or big equipment with chains or chokers should not be used. If you do use big equipment, leave more of the tree and hook on top of the extra.

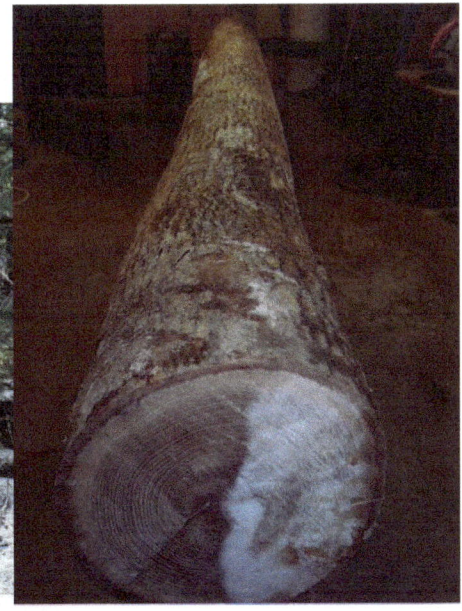

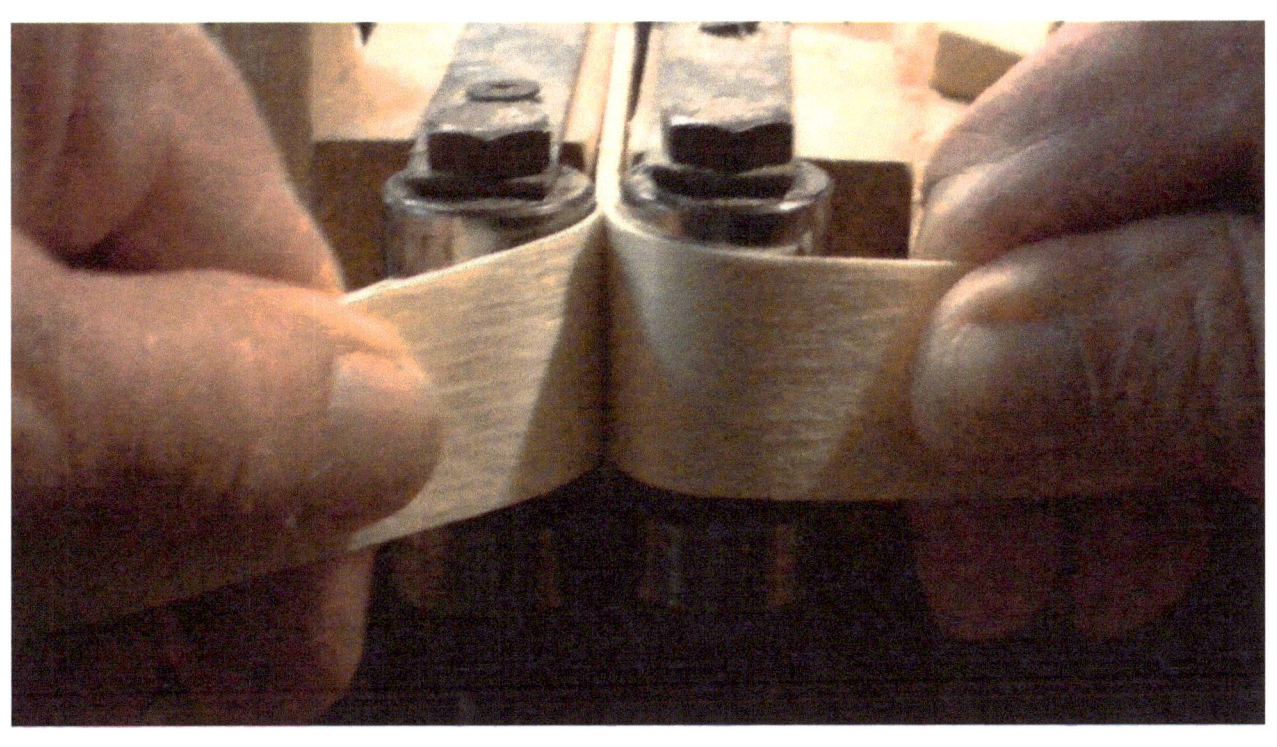

Note:

• CHAPTER 5 •

WOOD (BROWN ASH/BLACK ASH)

NOTE: Notches were used at times on the bottom of the tree to see how it was growing with an axe. Don't do this today because it may kill the tree. Some made 3" deep v knots on bottom side of the tree about 2' high.

The forests of Northern Maine include both coniferous and deciduous trees. The Brown (Black) ash tree has been the most useful tree for the Native Americans making baskets. Strong light containers of all types and shapes can be made with minimum experience and very few tools. With experience, baskets of great beauty can be produced.

For brown ash, location, location, location is the key. Good growing seasons, soil with water next to the roots, and fewer trees next to it for air space is what is needed. With straight bark marking and few knots is best if it tested and bends. Some to the best brown ash is on side of a hill but the roots reach water and the soil is fertile land with the right ph. A black ash tree was found in with the hard woods and was a great basket tree with no water around.

Please keep in mind as you continue reading that it is important to use good wood and materials to make an exceptional handmade basket. Everything is done for a reason. Do not get discouraged. Like anything, it takes practice to master any skill. Above all, follow the illustrations exactly as shown in the book. Take your time. The process will become easier and faster, especially after you have made one hundred baskets! Always keep safety in mind when doing each task. You never know when the unexpected will happen. Take your time and work the best you can.

ASH TREE TYPES

There are many types of ash trees. Brown ash (black ash) trees are common in northern Maine mostly next to water. Black or white-ash trees are a perfect wood for baskets. Since we make baskets that require strips of different lengths, we can use the wood below and above the knots. The outside of basket is the smooth side of the strip. Keep that in mind when working the tree.

The trees we use are called brown ash (Fraxinus nigra - Latin name). Brown Ash Trees, (also called black ash, swamp ash) are used because it has the most desirable properties. The branches are opposite, rather than alternate. They have pinnate compound leaves, meaning the leaves are opposite each other on a branch. They have five to eleven leaflets. Young trees have smooth bark. Some people make basket with white ash trees, but we don't.

When it is still green, the annual growth strips will separate more easily when pounded. This is because the glue that holds the rings together is weaker on the newer trees. The year's soft pores in between the growth rings can be separated. If the tree is growing well and thick enough, the layer can be split in two or threat times if thick enough.

Brown ash is the best natural spirit wood in the world to work with. It is a natural mate-

rial that is a all around us. Working the wood with care and skill, it can shape our lives in baskets and other products. It can help to enlighten our lives.

SELECTING THE TREE

Note: Always ask to cut tree, brown ash tree from the property owner. We trade or pay for the few trees that was picked for their quality.

We choose trees that are fairly straight and straight outside bark have a healthy look. We can see this by looking at the top and by looking at the bark grain going up and down the tree. The bark should not be twisted, and you want fewer knots. Warped grains will not work well. Find a good-looking tree with straight grain, few knots, and right size to handle. Six and a half

inches at the top is good, it's better for baskets if you can get a bigger tree with even growth thickness years.

A black (brown) ash tree should be twelve feet long is best and at least six inches in diameter at the top, with about ten to fifteen years of the sapwood. A good size tree, 12 inches in diameter by 12 feet long, can make over 50 good size baskets if is pounded on two notched logs.

This method will produce more baskets. It is usually a lot easier if you pound on the stick only. But you will not get as many baskets with this method.

Once we have tested the tree, it is ready for use. Don't use knots or wood that will not bend without splitting the grain out which will not work very well. Do not over beat your sticks either. This may smash the grain which will make the wood split. This will destroy the grain and pores. The natural glue within the tree will not be useable and will not last.

To make a quality product out of black ash strips or splints, weavers and uprights, the wood quality must be the best. This is something that is learned over years of working with this wood. Do not use wood with knots or wood that will not bend without splitting the grain. There may often be differences in the bending suppleness or quality of the wood even in the same tree. If the tree is not good for baskets, we use it for snowshoes, and if we can't use it for snowshoes at times have to still bend ok 4'we use it for a beautiful grained lumber.

Putting a tarp or plastic on or around the 6' to 12' log can help to drag the log out of the woods when there is snow on the ground pulling with a snow sled is also fast.

On a snow sled in the woods, you may need snowshoes to help pull it out. Snowmobiles or trucks may be another means to bring the logs to the workshop. Getting a bunch of trees at once is easier and saves a lot of time not having to go back and forth. It also good to remember that it is best to only get the number of trees you need for the year. Landowner will, at times, help you get the trees out with their equipment.

TESTING THE WOOD

Note: In the old days, an axe was used to make a small notch to see the growth. The tree was tested and left standing if it was not growing well. We find some of these trees at times.

Test the ash before making a basket is be very smart. Knowing what kind of flexibility of the wood quality, color, sizes of thickness and width is so important to the end product. Scrap-

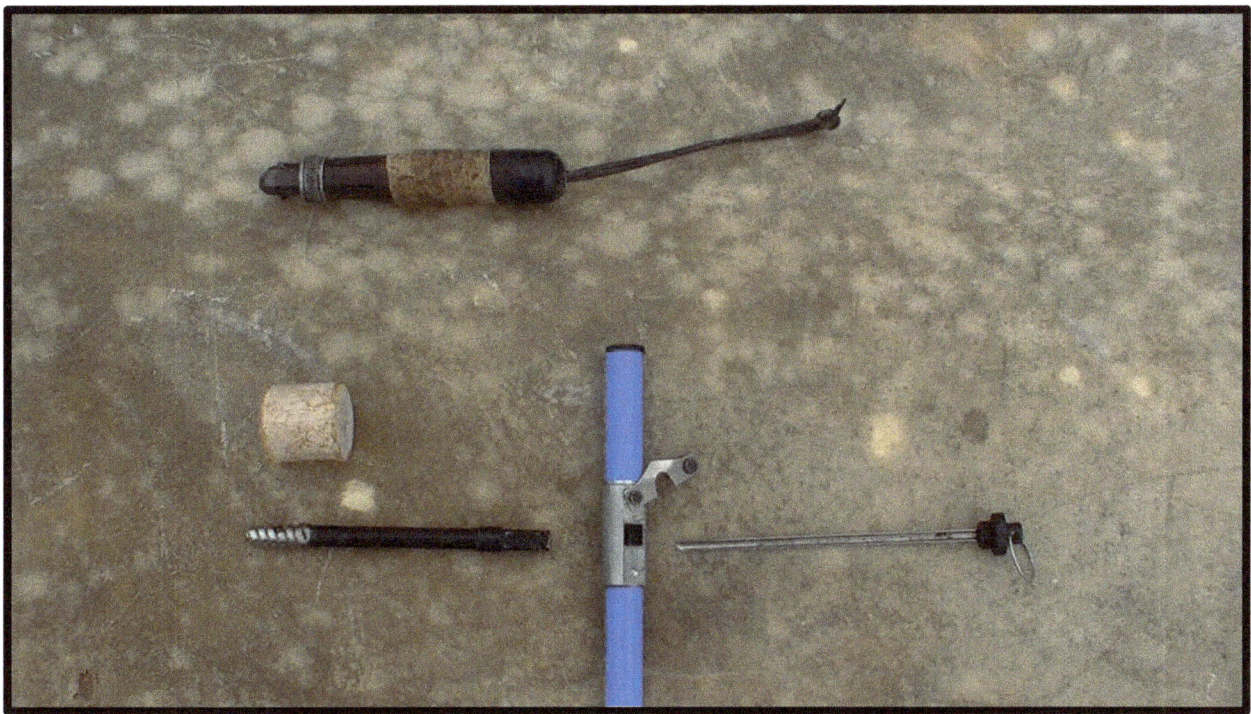

ing and or sanding are all relevant to what is going to be the end product. For example, potato baskets are to be good wood without the need of much sanding to give it the rugged look.

Testing is important before pounding a whole tree. Test it first before all that work is done. With an increment borer, we get a plug sample about 1 1/2-inch-deep on the east side of the tree to find out how the tree has been growing. The plug is taken out at a 90-degree angle to the tree at about 4 feet high on the east side. This is the first step for testing the tree. When ash is in small strips, test it for how straight and flexibility it is. This will tell how good the wood is. Cracking, snapping, and/or splitting are not good and working it will be harder. Different basket makers do it different ways.

Directions for Increment Borer

Borer Step

1: Put hollow drill bit and handle together.

2: Screw borer into the tree clockwise at 90°angle, about 1 1/2" deep.

3: Stick in '∩' shaped scoop all the way in.

4: Twist handle counterclockwise half a turn making the '∩' into a '∪'.

5: Pull out scoop with the plug inside of scoop.

   The length of the plug should be one and a half inches. The layers of the plug include the bark end white and brown hardwood sapwood. The sapwood of black ash is white, and the heartwood is dark brown. The greater the number of thick white rings found under the bark, the better the tree is growing. This plug does not hurt the tree; it will fill in with time. It is after examining a tree carefully, we cut it. Once the tree is down, we measure about 11 feet for the first cut. That length will be good for basket strips. The second cut is made 12 to 16 inches long at the top of the tree that is left for testing. This firewood length piece will be used to see if the tree will bend green so it can be pounded for baskets. This is also a test of flexibility. If the strip bends well, the tree will be good for baskets. If it cannot bend well, it is used for other purposes. That is the final test before we use the tree. (Note: black ash that is grown in swamps with cedar trees and other evergreens do not seem to bend as well as ash trees that grow in clusters with other ash trees. It also seems that, the higher up in elevation that the tree grows, the less pliable it is.)

   We have found that the tree bends better the closer you are to the stump or butt end. If a tree cannot be used for baskets or snowshoes, we have it sawed into beautiful grained lumber that can be used for furniture, snowshoe crosspieces, and racks. All the time, we are careful not to damage the outside of the tree. The remaining parts of the tree go into firewood.

   Wood with larger pores which cannot be seen with your bare eyes has more give and bends better. A good tree, that is growing well, can be bent green without steam. This retains the strength of the strips. The strength of the ash tree strips is in the layers of each year's growth and with the grain. Strips can be taken right off the tree with a skill saw. This technique is used the most by us because it is fast and easy.

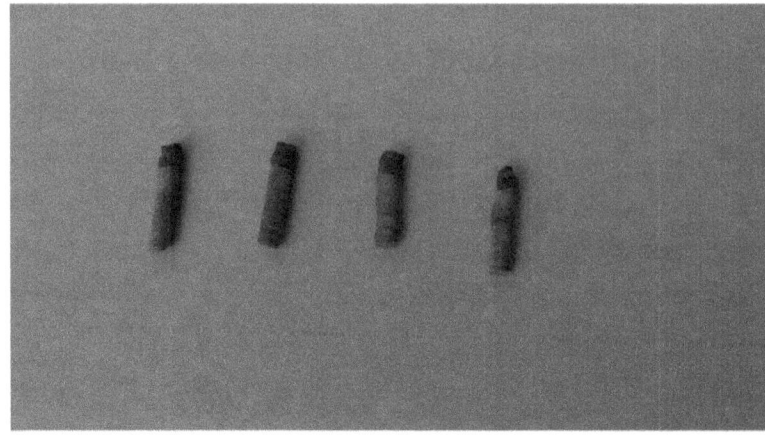

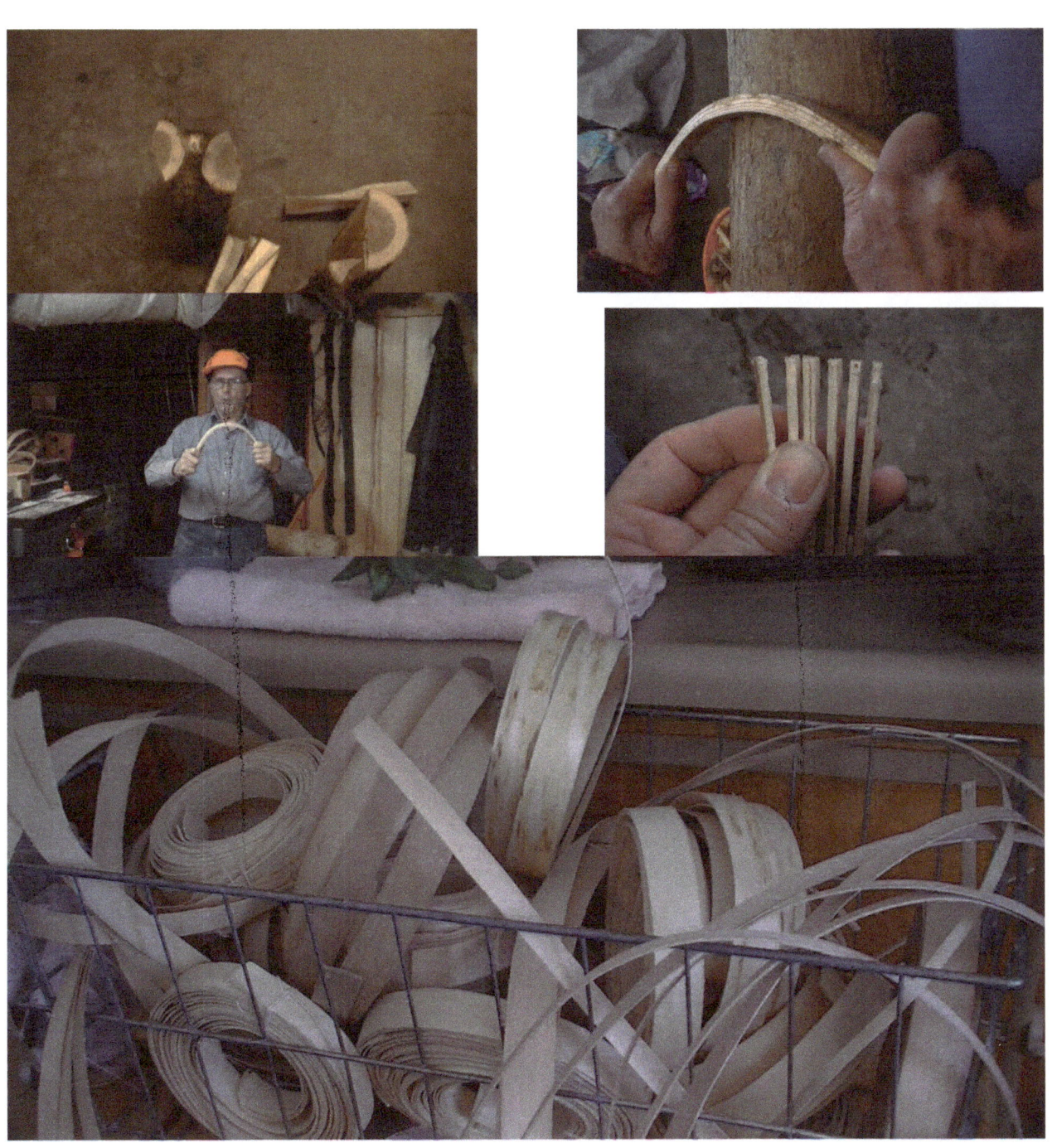

Start young, work hard, and keep traditions alive. Love what you do, put yourself into your art. Live your life as a Master artist.

STORING THE TREE

Fall is the best time of the year for harvesting tree logs of six feet and 12' long for baskets. We prefer to cut our trees in November, close to the time we will be using them. Six feet is what is needed for pack baskets for the uprights and all other baskets can use this length or shorter. Keep the log frozen until needed or wet in water. A pond with logs under water is best if you want to keep a long time in the summer. Cover the strips that are not used at once in the winter snow until needed. A cold place, under snow with a plastic covering is the best way to store the log in winter. A plastic sheet will hold the moisture in the wood. A tarp works well to keep the sunlight off. Keep your green wood away from the sun to prevent it from drying too quickly.

HARMFUL INSECTS

The Asian Long-Horned Beetle and the Emerald Ash Borer are two invasive insects that are working their way towards Maine which may be in Maine and Canada now these species are native to the Far East and were brought to North America with shipping materials. These insects are spreading throughout the New England area. The Asian Long-Horned Beetle feeds on hardwood trees, including maple, birch, poplar, and willow. The only way of eliminating this problem is by chipping or burning the tree that we know of so far.

Ash Bore Beetles (Emerald Ash Borer) are an enemy of all ash trees. The Emerald Ash Borer adult feeds on ash tree foliage, laying their eggs on the bark or in the bark. The young eat the sap wood under the bark. The larvae feed on the cambium under the inner bark, killing the tree. One concern is that they might be spread by transporting firewood. We need to keep an eye out for the Emerald Ash Borer because it has already caused extensive damage, killing tens of millions of ash trees in other states.

We want to keep them from moving into Maine, and we all play a part in keeping them out of North America. They are not native to the US. They bore under the bark in such a way that it will kill the tree very quickly. Please keep an eye out when cutting Ash trees and don't move the wood to different areas. The eggs or beetles can be easily spread. We need to report sightings to foresters or landowners because our forest ecosystem is at stake.

We want to do are part to protect this special tree because its special qualities give us the ability to bring other things to life once cut down. As of 2018, there were emerald ash borers found in northern Maine. It kills our ash trees which we use to make snowshoes, baskets, and other ash products. Keep an eye out for them. Report any bugs on ash trees.

Note: Keeping notes is a very good idea, because it can remind you later of what and how you progressed with your own ideas. This will also give others an opportunity to follow your technique.

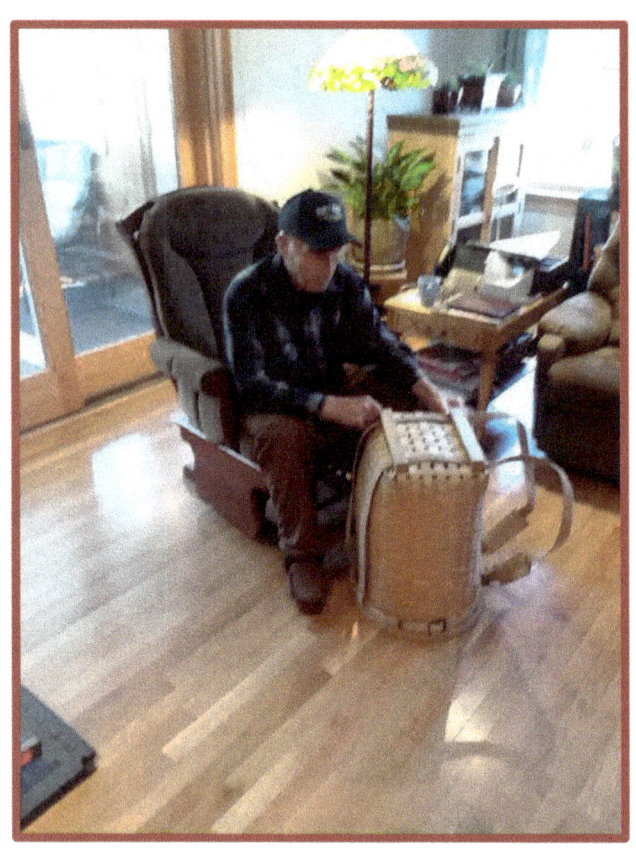

Notes:

Edmond Theriault and Benjamin Latvis

CHAPTER 6

WOOD WORKING

~ 92 ~

NOTE: **Ash trees must grow well to have the quality of flexibility that will not break or splinter out. This also allows the thicker layers to split more easily. And if it cracks and splinter out you don't want to use it because strips will start to fall apart faster.**

Working with your hands feels good to me, as my hands get harder and feel the wood between them, it is like going back in times were life depended on this art form. You can make round or square baskets once you have learned how to start them. Pounding ash logs is very hard work and will build up your arm muscles. After time, it will be easier. Practice makes perfect.

The outside of the tree just under the bark represent the first of the last year's layer of growth which makes for a very nice basket. Even using one layer around gives the basket a very nice look. We made a pack basket with only the last year layer with a little bark left for a nice color. This layer may also be used for many other things like rims and handles. The coloring makes the rim of the basket look good.

Only use the right thickness to match the size of the basket. The better ash bends well. Look at other baskets. The bigger the basket, the thicker the strips need to be. These sturdier pieces can also be used for up rights. Even the weavers must be thick at times. If they are too thin, the basket may be weak or have an inconsistent weave. The balance is very important and makes for a great basket maker.

*****

There are two main ways to get the weaving strips off the tree for making baskets. These two are the most common. The log can be pounded on as a whole or the log can be cut up into sticks. The log method takes longer and needs a lot of pounding to start loosening the layers. The stick method is more controlled, allowing the sizing of the width of the strips before the pounding starts. It also targets the pounding so that the layers separate more easily. Remember that you may need help to get a big tree out of the woods and into the workplace that's why we pick a smaller tree.

The longer you work with ash tree, the more you will learn about how it all works. Start with the right wood with the thickness, flexibility, color, moisture in the pounded strip, wetting the log by soaking it in water before pounding works best. A log rectangle pool of water, which you can make with a frame out of logs and plastic sheet on the inside can easily be made to store the log inside. The plastic will hold the water and is easy to move the pool around and change water. Keep turning the log every day until needed. You may have to change the water every week to keep log wood fresh.

LOG POUNDING TOOLS

NOTE: **Before pounding a downed ash tree, test the top end of the log extra foot piece with the back of an axe or a wooden mallet to loosen a strip. Peal it back and test for suppleness and flexibility. If the initial strips are of poor quality, it is a good idea to stop working on that log. Test some of your strips before you attempt to make your basket. It will save you a lot of work or reworking later.**

When pounding the log on blocks at each end, it works best if the log is twelve inches off the ground. Keep the log from moving or turning so the work surface is at the top. Make an ax "V" notch where the short log intercepts at a ninety-degree angle, close to each log end. This is the best height for pounding the log.

You can make your own pounding mallet of different sizes and lengths for specific applications. Mallets of different dimensions allow for different pounding pressures. It also helps with the convenience of diverse people. Although Hornbeam wood is not a big tree up north, it is an excellent wood to use for pounding mallets. It is a very hard wood that grows slowly. A two-handle axe, about three feet long with rounded edges on a big head, is also an ideal tool to pound with.

Sledgehammers, wooden mallets, or other choices should be easy to swing and bounce back. This is what will lessen the effort needed. Let the tool do the work. You just guide it as it drops and bounces back up. Control the tool as you create the momentum. At first, you might not find that your pounding has made a difference. Just keep going until the strip layers start coming off.

There is other poufnder tool made with motors that work well, but don't over pound with them, even when hand pounding over pounding can crush the grain and weaken your wood fibers making the basket weaker. You may not know why you are having a hard time with the basket falling apart or why the weavers breaking continually break. The fiber of wood is very important to the quality of the basket. It is important to pound the log just enough. The butt end of the log is the best with thick rings that can have more flexibility. Logs with fewer knots will make stronger baskets. Make sure there are no knots. Knots will show and make you basket look rickety.

Log Method

NOTE: Pounding in cool weather is more comfortable.

Cut the tree about six feet in length or longer. Place the six-foot log on end supports so it does not touch the ground. Take off all the bark and start pounding on the log with a mallet. When hitting the log, be it a horn bean wooden mallet or back of an axe let it bounce as it hit the wood. Hit all around the tree. Hit the log from the top to the butt mark and cut a strip to be pulled off. Use the axe the draw shaver, as needed.

It almost does it by itself once you are in your rhythm. Create drumming pattern while pounding, bouncing the mallet as you move over every part of the log. If the strip does not come off easily, you are not hitting hard enough. Hit hard enough to apply pressure. Keep turning the log a bit at a time, removing the same amount for each layer. It is important not to pound too hard. It is easy to over hit the indivisible strips. Let the tool do the work as you just guide it as it.

Pull off a few layers at a time. You cut a strip the width you want starting from the top and pull it off. If it doesn't want to come off keep pounding only on these spots that are stuck together. It will loosen and you will then see the strips come apart from the tree. Keep lifting on the strips until they come off.

After you have gone around the tree once, you should be able to take off the first layer. You will find the second time around will allow you to pull more layers at once depending on how hard you are pounding. The deeper you get the easier it is to remove the layers. Then start again, pounding until you hit the heart wood. These are the high-quality strips. It may take a day to prepare a six-foot log. This is the length needed for most pack baskets.

These strips can be cut for smaller baskets if needed. It is best to do as much pounding as possible as soon as you can to break up the strips. This is because the wood strips dry very quickly. Again, if you don't use all the stick, keep them wet, cold or under snow until needed. Make sure you give yourself time enough to do all that pounding at once. Do not be in great rush because you might make mistakes. Autumn is the best time to harvest your tree especially when the ground is frozen to move trees.

STICK METHOD

The second way is like getting strips for snowshoe frames. You use a skill-saw to cut a strip right off the tree. You make strip cut the width and depth you need and go around the tree. You then split the tree so you can remove the strips off the tree with the skill saw. As you move around the half tree you must change the angle and depth of the so you will not waste wood. You can only use about one half inch of the tree; you square the three sides on the table saw before

Jordan Theriault

pounding the growth rings apart as you have done on the round tree. You move the stick and pound on a stump or on something that is hard and doesn't move. Your strips will all be the same width. You can now roll the strips and tie them in rolls that will easily fit in the container you will be soaking them in before using.

I prefer the stick pounding, less pounding, faster result, easier to identify each layer, easier to size after, control grain run off. Cut wide parts picture. Keep the grain straight and fiber going all same way when trimming the wider edges. Sanding with a 4 ½" hand powered grinder with soft backing and sandpaper afterwards keeps the runoff from splinter out.

STEPS FOR MAKING STRIPS

1. Make sure log is at right height for taking bark off. You can adjust it for your height.
2. Cut strips around the tree after taking the bark off.
3. Spit the tree.
4. Move the other half until needed.
5. Putting the sticks on the table so they are not on the ground. You do not want to bend down all the time. Also, the mess is not so much in your way.

CUTTING STICKS

NOTE: You can sometimes get as many as 16 sticks about one inch wide and one and a half thick in about a per 9" inch diameter Log.

Cutting frozen logs works best wait the next day to split the log and remove the sticks. Once the tree is back at your workshop, place the tree at a comfortable height off the floor on rounded short, ∪ shaped top sawhorse that has been prepared in advance. Taking the strips off the tree is done preferably on a cold morning, when the tree is partially frozen. We use a radial

saw (8" skill saw) for this job, and it seems the blade does not gum as much if the tree is frozen. It also keeps the blade cool.

With a drawknife, remove about half the thickness of the bark for a four-inch wide strip on top of the tree to check for knots or other defects. The bark that is left remaining will keep the strips from drying once they are off the tree. The lighter white sapwood growth rings go around the outside of frames. Split the tree to get the strips off. Once it has been sawn, cut around the outside of the log. If there is an increment borer hole or knot in the tree, start the first cut right next to it.

Throw a line if the tree is straight or just stay on top of the tree with the skill saw. Always start from the top sawing towards the butt of the tree, cutting 1 3/8 to 1 1/2 inches deep. After the first cut, turn the tree slightly to make a second cut 1 1/4 inches from the first cut at the top. Turn the tree after every cut to stay on top of the tree. (Remember the butt end diameter of the log is always greater.) Remove more bark after every two cuts to give the saw a break. Never push the saw blade to go faster than saw blade can handle it without overheating. This will prevent overheating. You keep cutting, peeling, and turning until you have gone around the tree. Use a long flat chisel to help pull frame strips off following the saw cut.

Continue around the log until finished. The log is now ready to be split in two. It is easier to start at the top of the log and make a second half inch deeper cut in the same two cuts where you will start splitting the log. Start the split at the top of the log with a thin ax head or wedge. As the split opens, use other wood wedges made of 2 inches by 4 inches, 12 inches long. Also, an old axe head or metal wedges can be used on the log until there are two split pieces of the log. It is easy now to remove the strips off the open half log with the skill saw. Be careful not to cut

too deep. This may damage the strip under the one being taken off. Make needed adjustments as to depth and angle as you go along. The depth and the angle of the skill saw may have to slightly change as you move from the inside of the half log the more strips that are done, the easier to learn how to set the blade and how to pass the saw. The inside can also be used, making big trees more useful.

Removing strips from a log takes about one hour. Some other tools, such as a small axe to cut the strands holding the tree together, may be needed to help remove the strips off the half logs. Be careful not to spoil the wood. The tree must be green and not frozen to split it. Grain, which might run out every which way, will make you lose some strips. Use steel toe boots for protection when working with a log, chainsaw, or any sharp tool that may drop on to your foot.

Green wood is always the best because it bends easier, but you may have to tighten more when weaving. Picking wood that bends more easily is best because it will be easier to make baskets. You can tell the quality of wood by the splinting out of the weave or breaking at sharp bends which is not good. When you look at it in your hands and work with it, it will tell you the quality of the wood. When the strips pass through your fingers, you can tell the thickness and roughness of the wood and how brittle it will be when bending. Check out the strip for knots and defects that you may not want them as part of the basket. I like to do a lot sorting and sizing of the similar pieces right away. This will make it go faster when you move to making the basket.

The strips can dry, and it happens very fast. If you don't use all the sticks at once, keep them wet, cold, and under snow until needed. Make sure you give yourself time to do all the pounding at once and you're not in any rush where mistakes and harm to someone happens. Fall time is best to get the tree, with frozen ground to move the tree, some snow will help.

When trimming the wider edge of the log or sticks, keep the grain straight and fiber all going in the same direction. Sanding with a 4 ½" hand powered grinder with soft backing and using sandpaper afterwards will limit runoff from splintering out on the sides of sticks. Please make sure you pass the grinder quickly over the wood so as not to burn the wood.

Once the strips are shaped on the table saw, they are now ready to be start pounding. When waiting a few days, wrap strips in plastic to keep them from drying.

POUNDING STICKS

NOTE: Do not use about fifteen inches of the stump since this section has a faster growth making the strips thicker at that end. It is best to do as much pounding as soon as you can to break up the strips because of the drying that happens with open wood

It usually takes two people about 3 to 5 minutes per stick if struck in a good way, to get about 16 pieces of weaver and or up rights per stick six feet long. With two people working together, one person can hold the stick and the other can pound it. Hit on top covering all the stick surfaces topside under side and turn it back around to the top side pounding and do the same at the angle about 45 degrees. You can switch people positions with each stick, simply pound on the top for the length of the stick. Then turn over and do the same. The start of the pounding may require a few more hits. Pound a strip from one end to the other until the year's growth rings separate. Then when it falls apart and starts to make a snapping noise you can keep moving at the same angle while the other person hitting always on the edge of the wood strip. This requires practices and focus because you don't want to slip and cause injury to the other person. (Wear leather gloves to hold the stick is the best way to protect your hands).

Develop a good trust between yourself and the other person with whom you are working with. Be aware of the vibrations the pounding produces. When you get close to the end of the stick turn the stick around and do the same at the angle and keep on hitting. You may want to give a few more hits first on the flat top and bottom to make it easy for it to come apart. The person holding the stick should have good leather gloves. Be sure to hold the stick firmly on you work surface. When bending the log on blocks it will work best if the log is 12 inches off the ground from the top of the log to the work surface. Keep the log from moving or turning. When trimming the wider edges, keep the grain straight and fiber all going in the same directions. By sanding with a 4 ½" hand powered grinder with a soft backing and sandpaper afterwards will keep the runoff from splinting out keeping this in mind.

It's important to remove the strip apart as soon as they are loose, even if more force is needed to separate them to get them out of the way. There are a lot of tricks to making baskets, but once the knowledge is gained, it is that much easier. Make sure the length of the materials used is long enough. Using the blunt back end of a axe or wooden mallet is all that is needed, The best way to loosen the year's growth to make baskets. Control the pounding and do it just right, being careful not to ever pound it. As you take a few layers off, pull appart the layers by hands.

Try not to over beat your sticks or it may smash the grain and pores in the wood. This may make it unusable. Once again, keep in mind that strips of the same thickness and widths are for the best baskets. The best wood should be sorted and always bent inward. The wood should always be natural, just as it comes off the tree, then bent inward when weaving a basket. It be pounded with whatever being a back of axe head or wooden mallet or long handle mallet or by some kind ash pounder machine, I have made my own pounder with help, putting together but with my design. Which use square strips are pounded but I have seen a whole tree pounder also.

SPLITTING STRIPS

NOTE: If you are going to make better baskets, you should split the strips that are thick and scrape the sides that are rough when the strips are fresh before you put them in storage.

Some very thick layers can be spilt again using a splitter tool. Doing it free hand is okay but takes time and a lot more skills. Only good thick growth rings are spit. It may even be spit again if it really thick, if it is thick as a nickel it can be split. Usually one spit is good and will work well. Going slower is always the best way to start learning how to split the splints in half. (Pressure is key, moving the strip when splitting for control for even sides of the splint).

Splitters have been made which makes the job easier but pulling both sides evenly is still the struggle. The splitter in use consists of a board about three feet long and four inches wide with a slot in the side that comes out at the end. The board is held between the knees with the end on the floor. The Ash strip is passed through the side up to the top where it is split and started then with both hands you pull each side of the strip down splitting it.

Splitting on the knee is okay but should be done very carefully. The strips are split by hand by cutting the strip about the halfway with a sharp knife and starting to separate the strip in two. The trick to splitting a strip is pulling on the inside and outside of the strip evenly. By pulling more on one side you will find that side will get thinner. Splitting a strip is easier if it is about one inch wide or less.

Our homemade splitting tool works best because you can control the splitting. We have made a splitter where we split the Ash strip on the side so we can see better if the strip is going close to the middle and not going more to one side as we pull sideways. Put two boards together with a workspace. And even connect the splitting by flipping it. If the split is not running straight, this tool will help to control your splitting. It is faster and easier to use and works great.

Place your knife at a slight angle on the wood while resting it on a good size thick piece of leather on your knee. Pull the split ash strip between them and pull with your other hand. Go slow to start. Then, once the knife is placed on position where it works best, go more quickly with caution. A very sharp knife will work best. The use of a utility knife at times may be utilized if it starts to stick and run off. The ease of the process will depend on how sharp you keep your knives.

The split strips are very special wood that is silky on the inside between a year growth. There is another older traditional way of splitting that works, but it requires more skill.

This helps when pull the split which at times I will at flip the strip which may split better then another, and time may have flip many times and help it a bit with the tip of the utility knife, which is another control of the splitting.

Once you cut around the log, look at the two lines that match up the best and cut deeper, this is for the splitter split all over the places. Cutting frozen works is best around the log and then waiting the next day to split log and then to cut off the stick. (Always cut from the top of the tree to the butt of the tree).

SCRAPING

You can scrape the rough sides and if the layer is thick enough. Scraping the outside of the ash strips before starting the basket is best. We make a scrapper with a ball bearing on top of a blade. The bearings help to reduce friction. It works well and is very safe using both hands. When one side moves and the other side with bearing doesn't move, for better control for splitting. Our tool is faster and easier to use. We think it works great! Ball bearing rollers sees picture will give you the very best control, with less effort. If it gets stuck, take a sharp knife and run it back in half. Monitor this closely so that you will start to lose you even split and must start over again.

Using the under the arm method to assist your hand with long bending works well. Remember, not all ash wood bends the same. A trick is to work a big bend many times to achieve a smaller bend. If you want to have it bend and not break, special care is needed. This is an old trick that makes the difference between a good bend and a not so good bend. Some wood needs to be worked more, back and forth, many times until it gives. Some wood is just not any good, so don't worry about it, simply move on to another piece of wood. Again, green ash wood is the best wood to bend because of its flexibility. However, bending it can be tricky. Bending it a little bit time works best.

How ash wood is and where are just as important to bending ash. If steaming the ash wood is what needed, it means doing another step which up to you. We just don't like to do another step. This is not done for baskets as far as I know. It may be used for handles. Ash trees have to grow well and have the quality of flexibility that will not break or splitter out. The thicker ones can be split easily in two or thick enough for three, which is quite thick and harder to do.

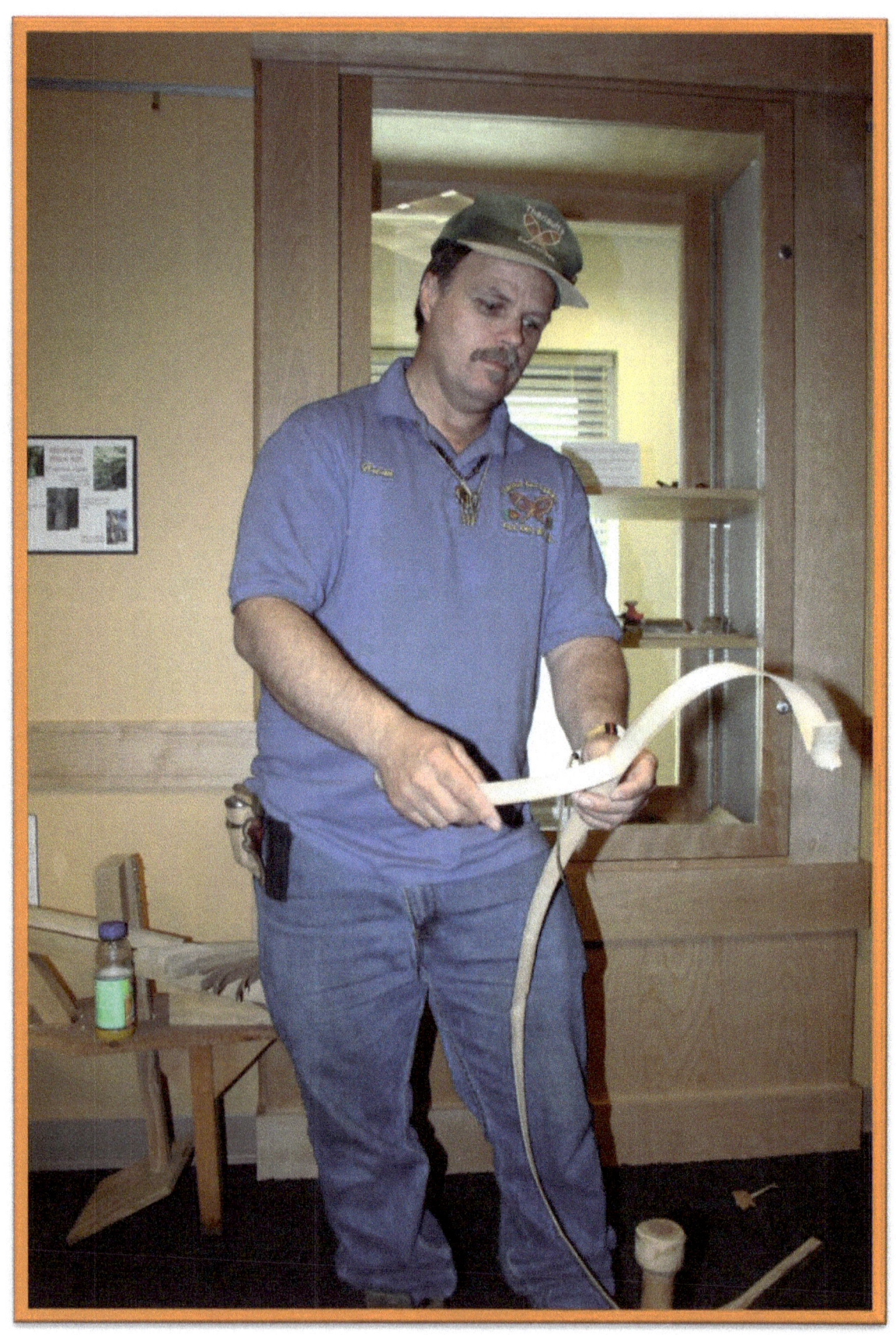

Storing strips

Note: Sanding or scraping before putting strips in the rolls is easiest when the wood is green. It is very important that the strips remain flat. Ash strips are strong and can be used to tie things together.

As best as you can, place the unfinished strips as much as you can in tight rolls of no more than a foot in diameter. Smaller roll is easier to store and handle best. Use working strips right away.

Storing your strips is very important until you are ready to start weaving. When the pounded strips are ready to be put away, rolling up is the best way to do this. The rounded ash strips are flatter when done right, which is needed when you want to use them to make baskets. This should be done right away once you pounded all the tree or sticks from the tree. You want the outside of the tree side to be flattened, so that it is now on top or outside the roll. Four or five strips can make a good size roll. Tie with a white twine. Show pictures

One of the keys to making baskets with ash strips or the press with weight to leave it flat and in shape will drying having pressure. Making a press width wood metal to be placed with cardboard first with a flat surface then weight and leave it there for a week so it will dry very well, and you can now put a finish on if you want. By rolling the ash tree you are keeping them flat and easily to handle and put into a small container of water when needed.

Keep all strips organized so it is easier to find what you need. Making an organizer can help you find the layers you want to work with. There should be 16 to 20 places to keep it all same thicknesses together. Labeling the rolls with how good they bend, and lengths is also helpful. Separate the ones used for rims and the rough scraped ones. The widths and lengths can be used to separate pieces. Keep them together and marked. Fasten the rings on two sides very tightly together while keeping the bark side of the tree facing out. It is very important the strips remain flat. Store your strips in a dark dry place like in a paper bag and it will last much longer. Place in brown paper bags, flat one on top of another and move them all around every once and while. They should be stored in a dry place in your house.

Your rolls should be of a size that can be soaked in warm water to make the pliable again. You soak them in water when you are ready to use them.

When making baskets, you want your strips flat, not curled because they may later flatten and cause your basket to loosen. A loosely woven basket frame is not very usable. It will quickly become unstable causing the weave to come apart. This will take away from the appearance. Any time you don't finish your basket, reroll the strips you didn't use to keep them flat and easy to rewet as needed.

Your test trips will really tell you information. Just pay attention to the splitting and if it with the grain. Again, don't use bad strips or bad ash tree because it will always take time to fix strips and make for a bad basket. Cut off strands or fibers that may be hanging off the main strips. If you just pull on it, you may pull off more than you wanted. With a knife you can trim off a little piece that may snag.

I have found that dry rolls of black ash strips can be easily to work if soaked for a few days to a week checking their suppleness daily depends on how dry they are. Keep checking it every day once it is cut into the shapes you want it to bend. When cut into shape, you want them to bend easily. You still may have to flex the ash strips a few times depending on how thick the wood is. Flex each strip slowly from the thinner end toward the thicker end. Working it to achieve an overall big bend in each strip and then tighter. In time you will feel how the wood wants to bend. Some woods will bend easily. Others will require more technique in your hands.

Your test strips will become a good "teacher"! The rounded ash strips are flattened before using to make baskets. This should be done right after you have pounded the layers from the tree or sticks. You want the outside of the tree side to be flattened, so it should be rolled in a way it is now on top or outside the roll. Four of five strips can make a good size roll. And tie with white twine.

    Placing them into a paper bag or paper boxes help keep things organized. Leave room to close the bag and store in a dry place, where temperature is close to room temperature. Mark or tag the outside of the bag so it will ready to use and you will know what you and the right conditions for the strips. Keeping all the same kind of strips together helps. Indicating what the length and how many are in the bag will help to make a good basket. Keeping track of quality is important. Once you have had a bit of practice, you will find it helpful to keep enough of the different strips for a basket in one paper bag. Some baskets need thicker uprights and you don't want all kinds of strips drying. You don't want lose pieces which end up getting dirty and you will have to throw them away because you won't be able to use them to make a beautiful basket.

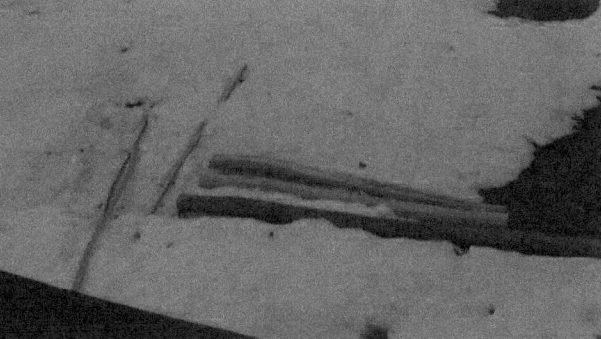

DYEING, COLORS

Note: No splitting or scrapping once the pieces are dyed. You need to dye all the ash strips in the sizes you need to make the basket. If you cut or scrap it, will show up and will not look good.

Contrasting color strips can be added once the basket is finished to extend the wear and enhance the design. Dyeing the white strips to different colors makes for really beautiful baskets. In the old days they used any type of natural dyeing agents, from blood to bark, berries and soil.

Glass jars in clean water work very well for dyeing strips. The lid with a seal in place, there is less evaporation, keeping the consistency of the dye the same. With ash strips that are dry and rolled up, place them loosely into the dye. You also can put the ash strips into water until it is wet which may take a few hours. Then you can put it into the cool dye. When finished with the dye, place the cooled dye into a big glass jar, like a pickle jar with a cover until needed again.

The color of ash will change over time and all will darken in time while dying. However, the color of ash strip may lighten over time, especially when in the sun. You can soak the brown strips in bleach to make it whiter which then you can dye them to the color you want. You can roll up dye strips and tie up, until needed again. Warm water and change the water every day will help at times. Leaving strips in water for long times will darken the strips; you still must keep changing the water if you want the darker brown color. You will have to presoak in water before using again.

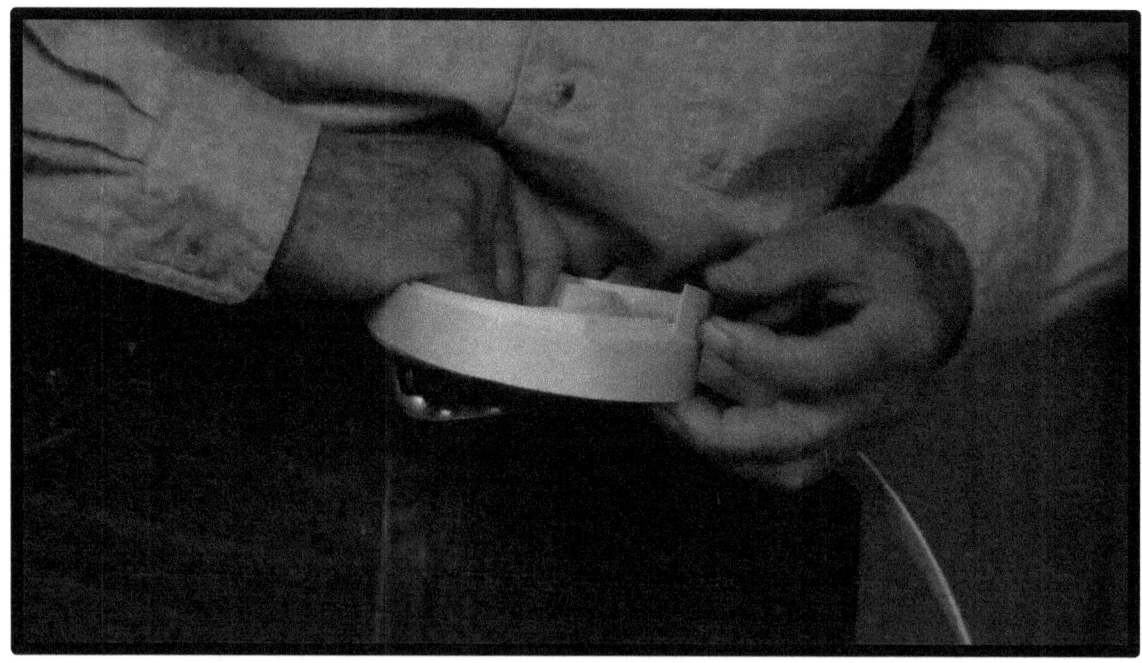

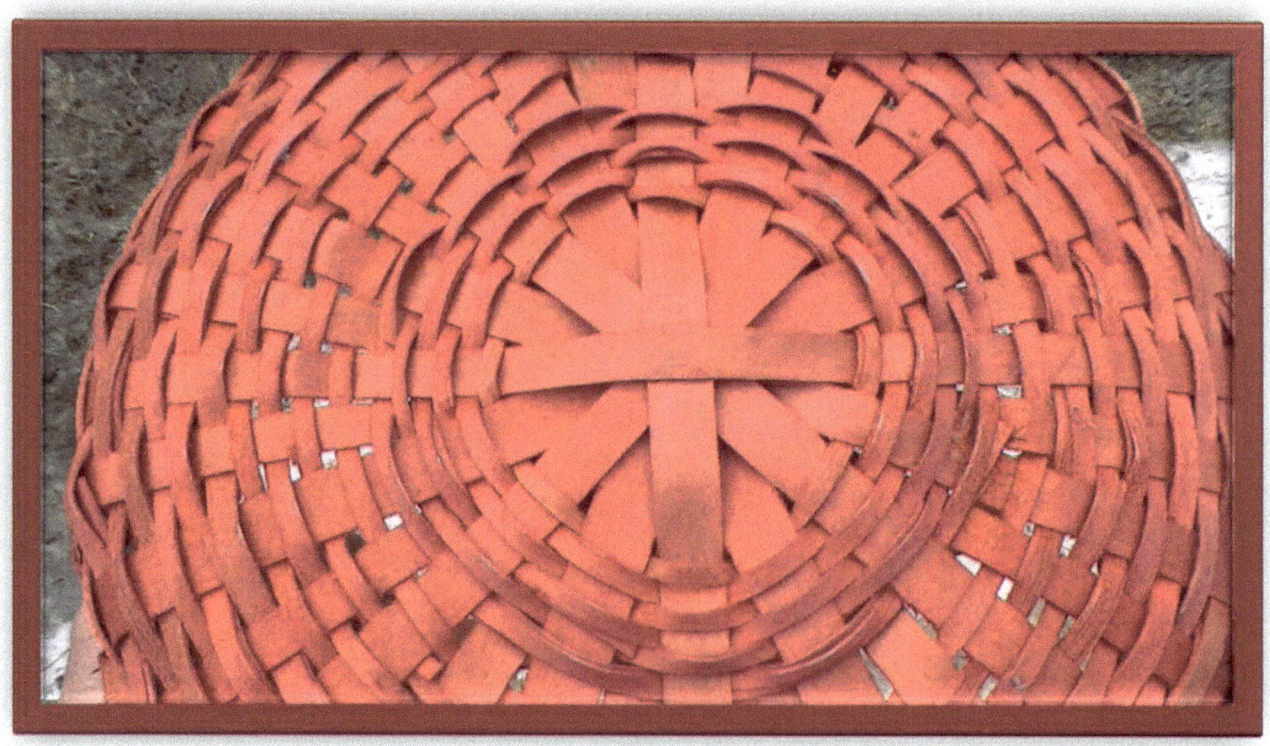

DYEING: BY JOAN THERIAULT

Beats were used to dye wool and dying material like ash strips for baskets. There is instruction on the boxes of dye you buy at the store. Powder was the old way of selling dye, which is okay, but now they have liquid which is better and easier to use.

1. Boil water in a big stainless-steel metal pan. Then add the dye in at this time. Turn the stove off. Do not use these pans for cooking any more.

2. Once the water is cool, put the green ash strips loosely in the pan so the dye can go all around the ash strips. If they are in a roll tied up, you must cut the string and make the ash strips loose.

3. Leave the ash strips in the dye until you have the right color, the intensity you desire. It may take a half hour or so to get your color. Rinse the ash strips until the water is clear in another container. This is very important. Remove ash strips and damp dry on rags. Working on the basket at this time while it is still wet or moist might be a good idea. If the strips dry out, you must dampen it with water to keep working on the basket. Using a spray bottle of water works well.

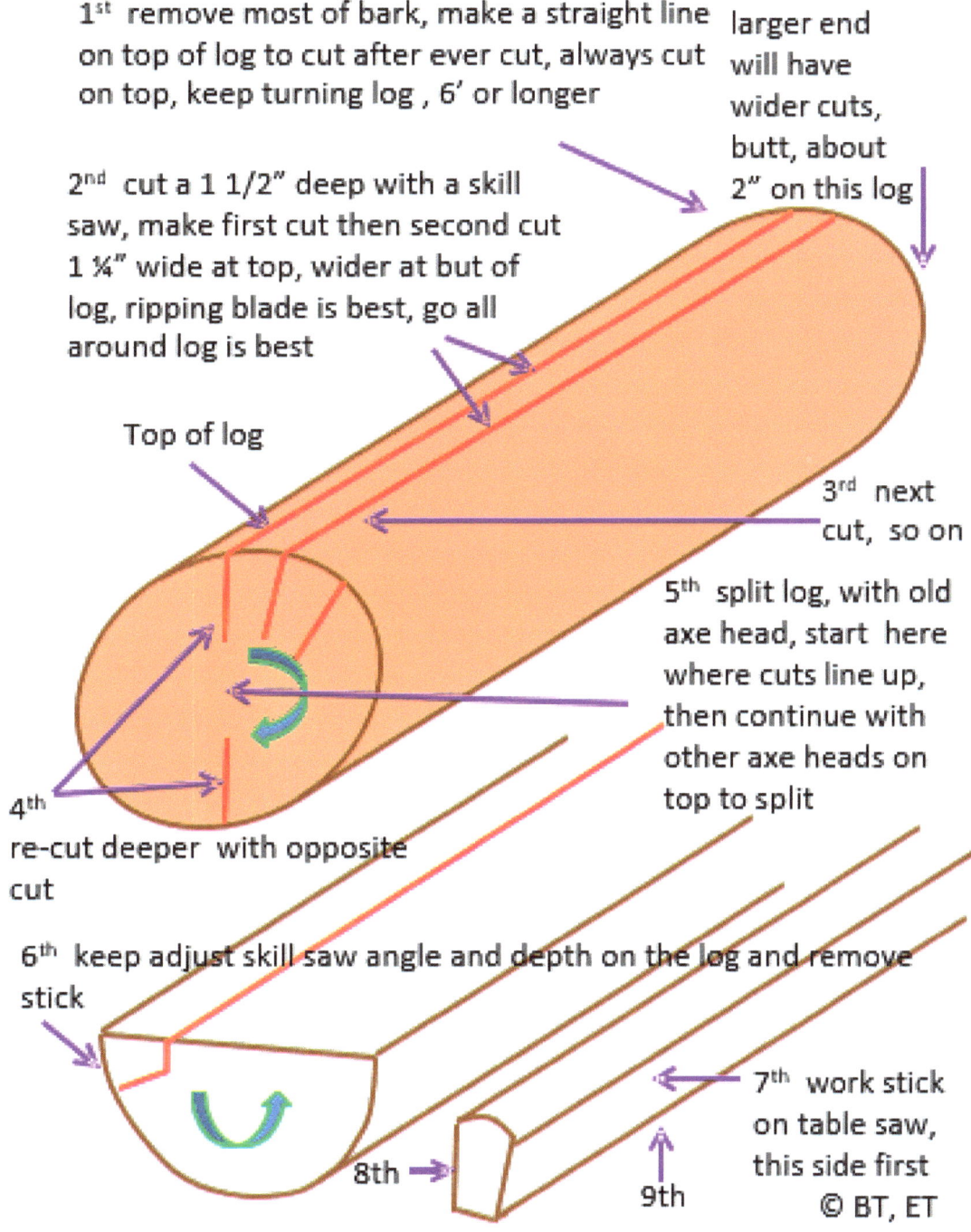

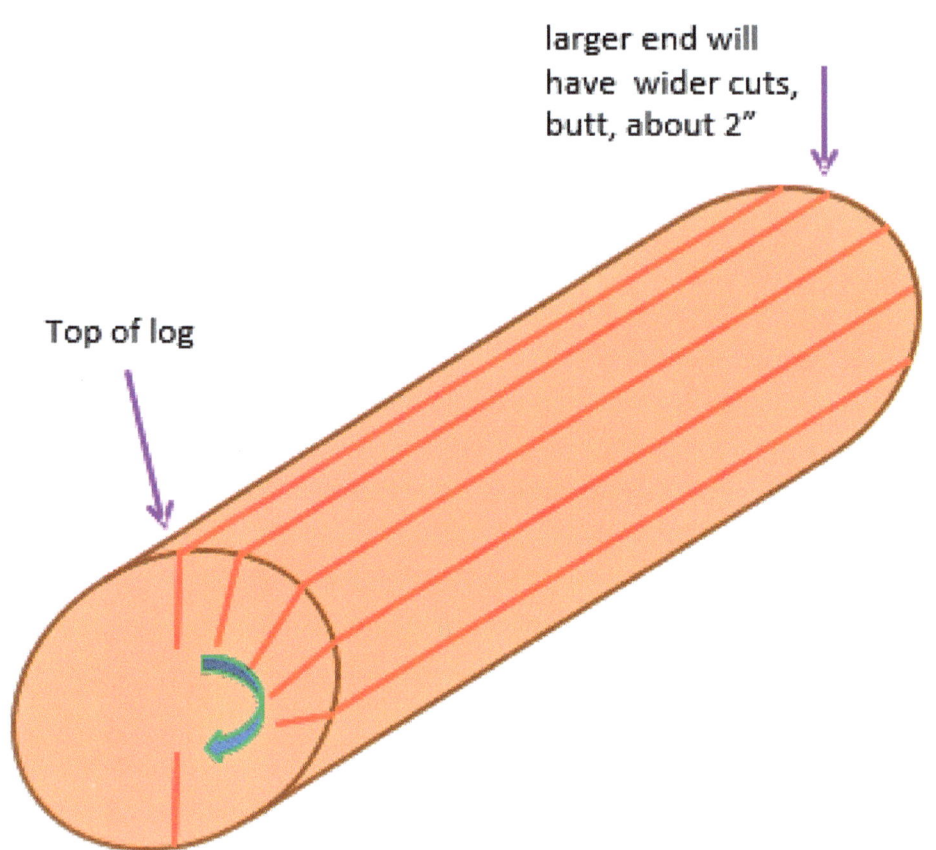

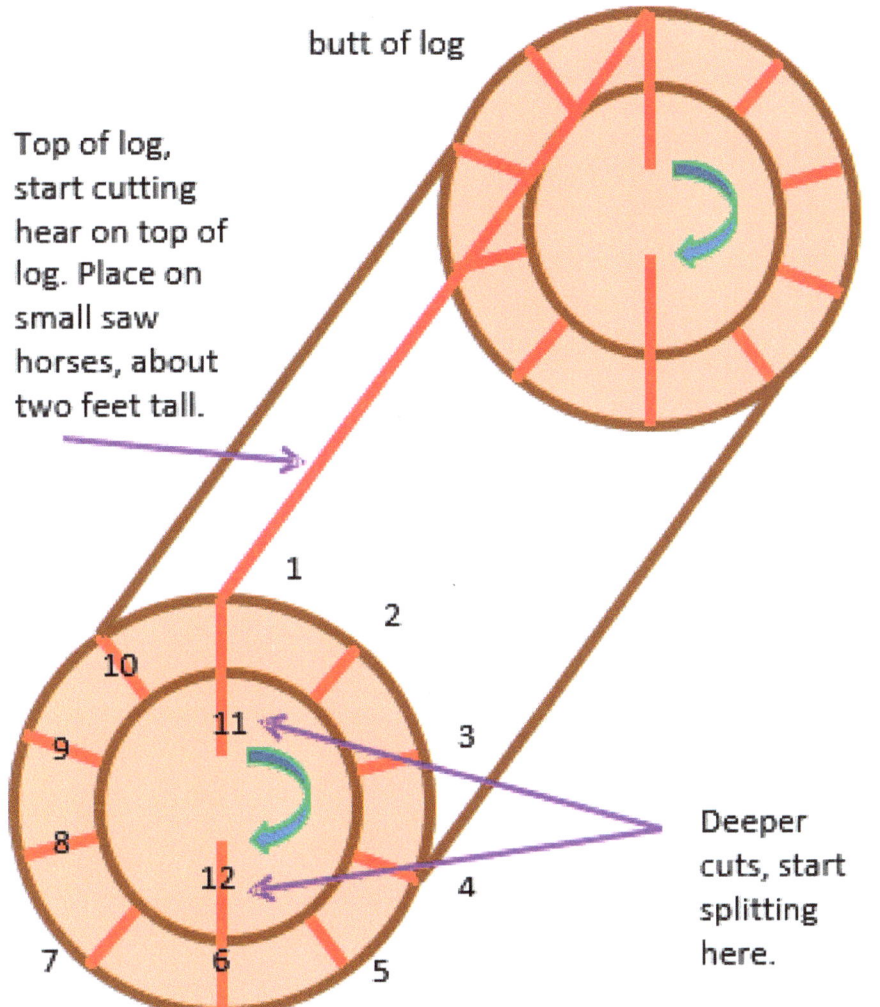

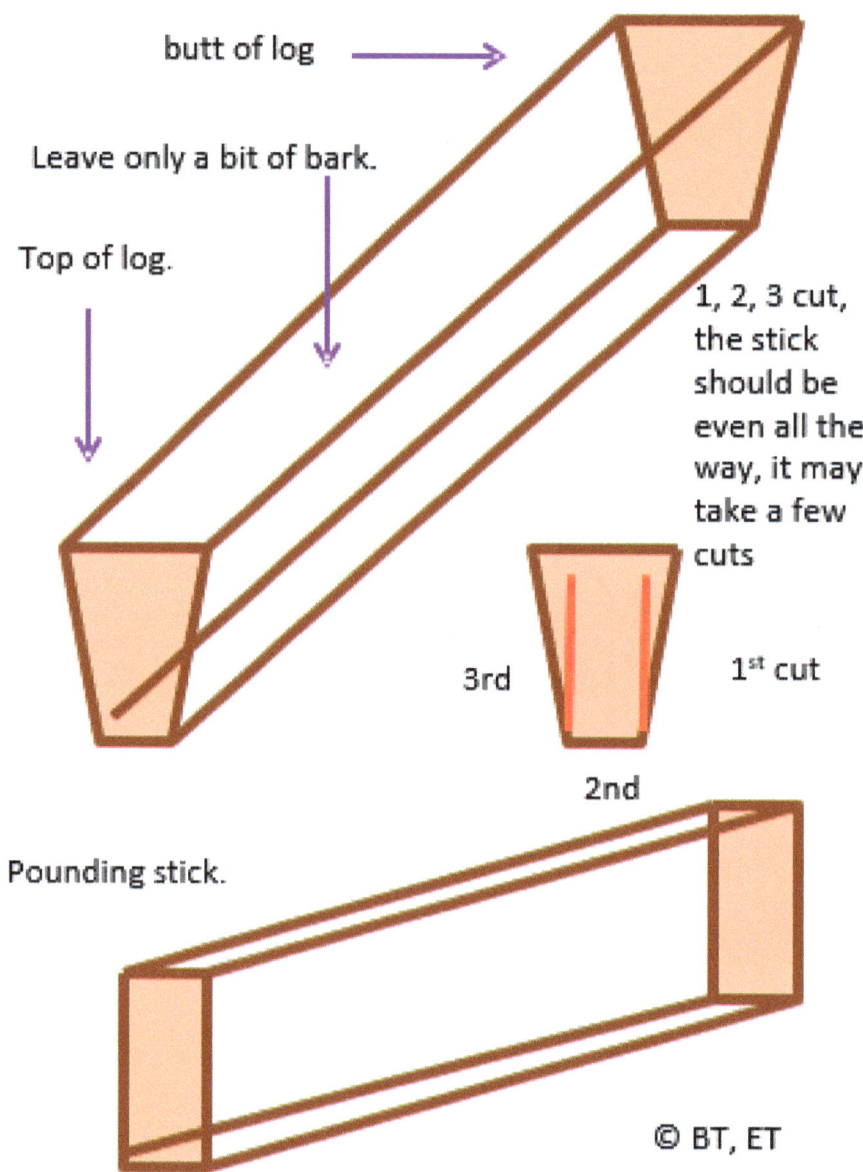

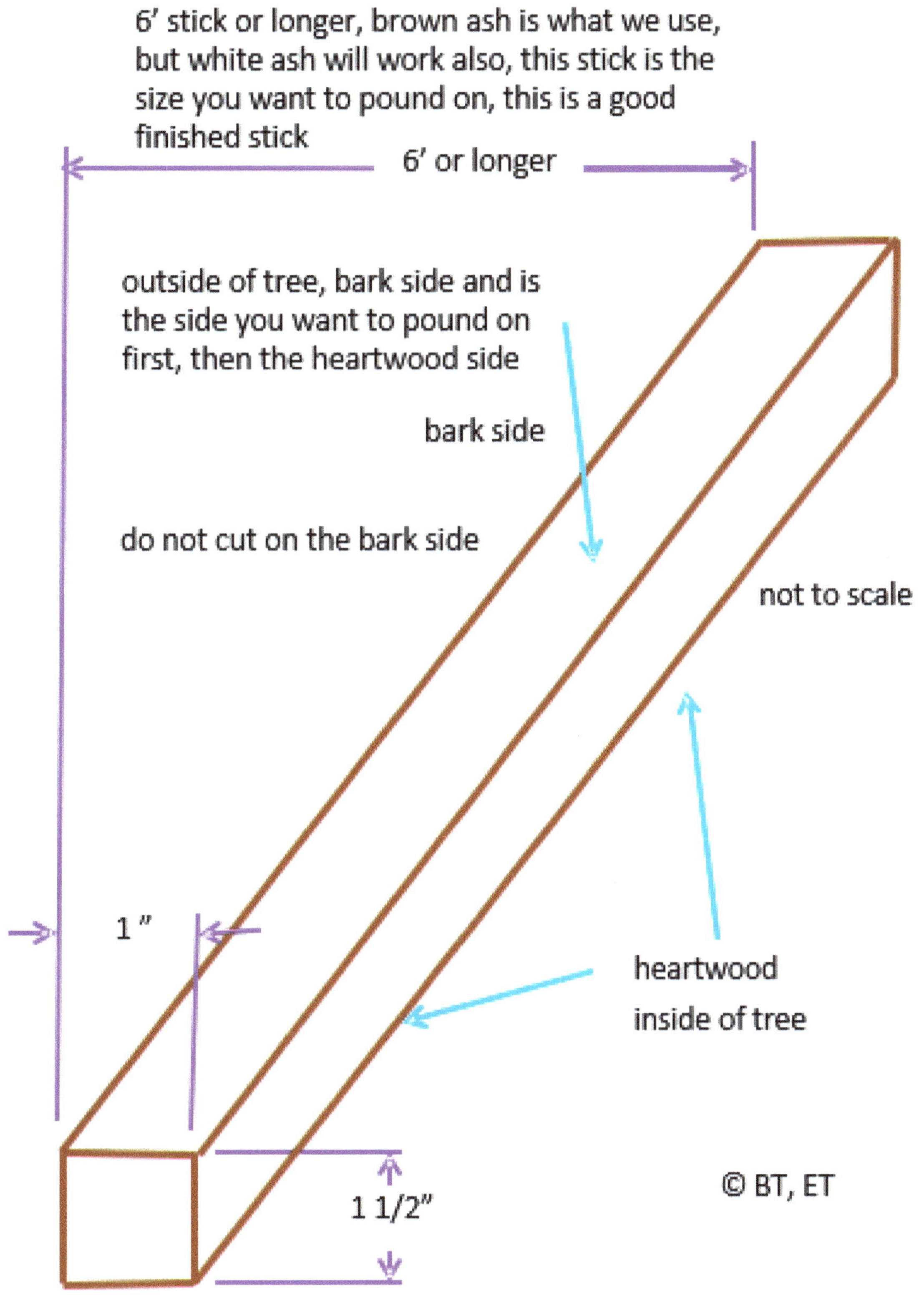

6' stick or longer, brown ash is what we use, but white ash will work also, this stick is the size you want to pound on, this is a good finished stick

6' or longer

outside of tree, bark side and is the side you want to pound on first, then the heartwood side

bark side

do not cut on the bark side

not to scale

1"

heartwood
inside of tree

1 1/2"

© BT, ET

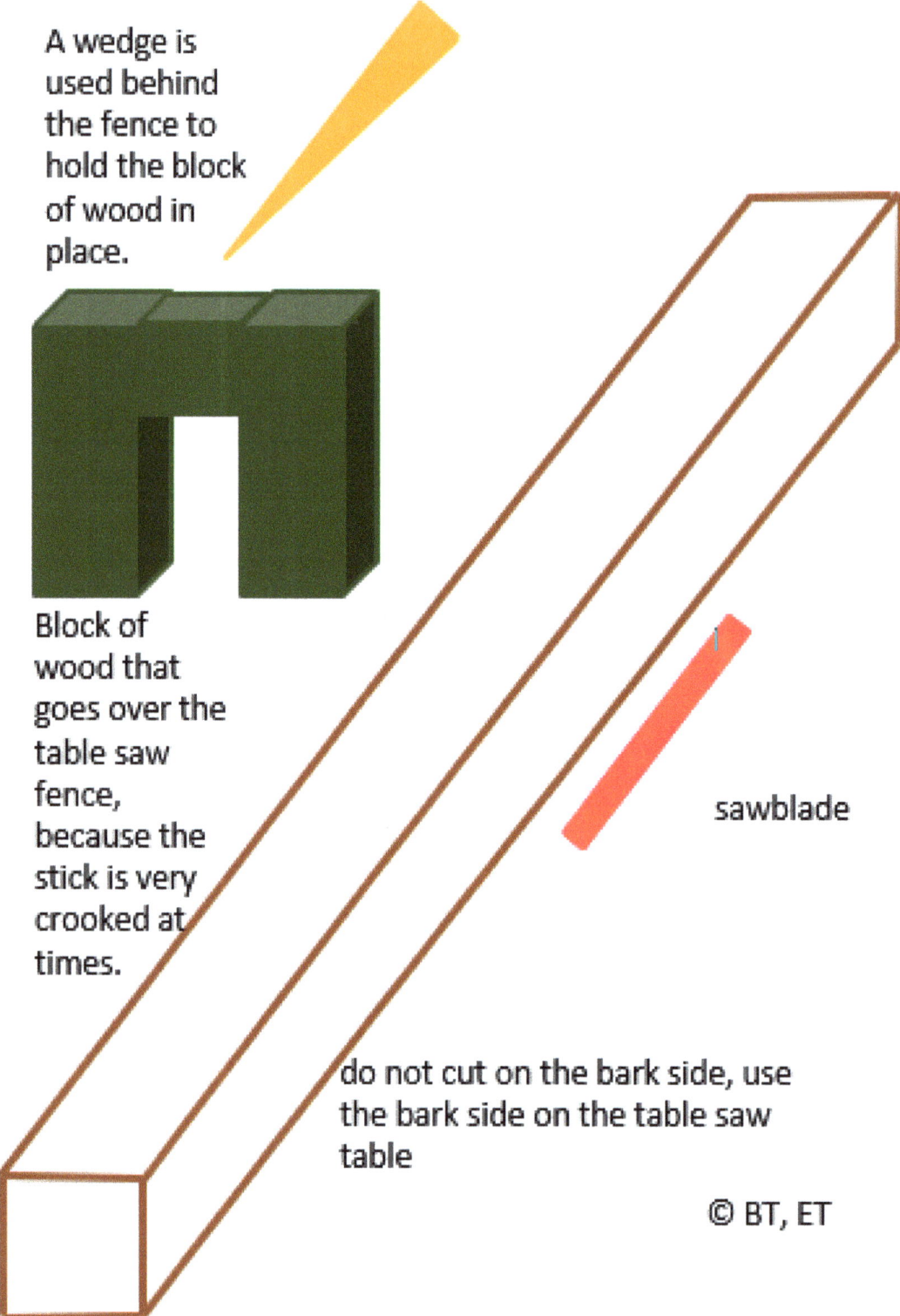

A wedge is used behind the fence to hold the block of wood in place.

Block of wood that goes over the table saw fence, because the stick is very crooked at times.

sawblade

do not cut on the bark side, use the bark side on the table saw table

© BT, ET

Basket wood is a gift to us to used for so many unique, and meaningful useful, and still so treasured today.

1-9

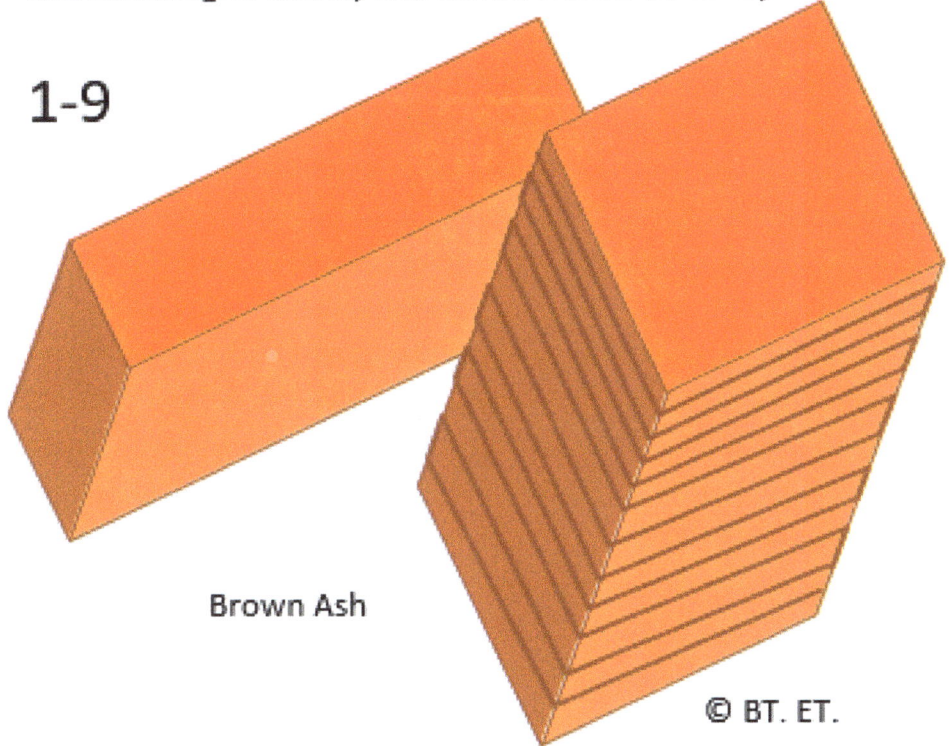

Brown Ash

© BT. ET.

The glue between the years growth rings is not so strong when the tree is still green and the first few inches of the sap wood is the best material. The pours or little holes are easily crushed or pounded or sharp bending will let the years grown come apart.. There are many way to accomplish this which you may even invent your own way. The key is to get the right tree to begin with.

Basket tree wood is a gift to us which is still so treasured today.

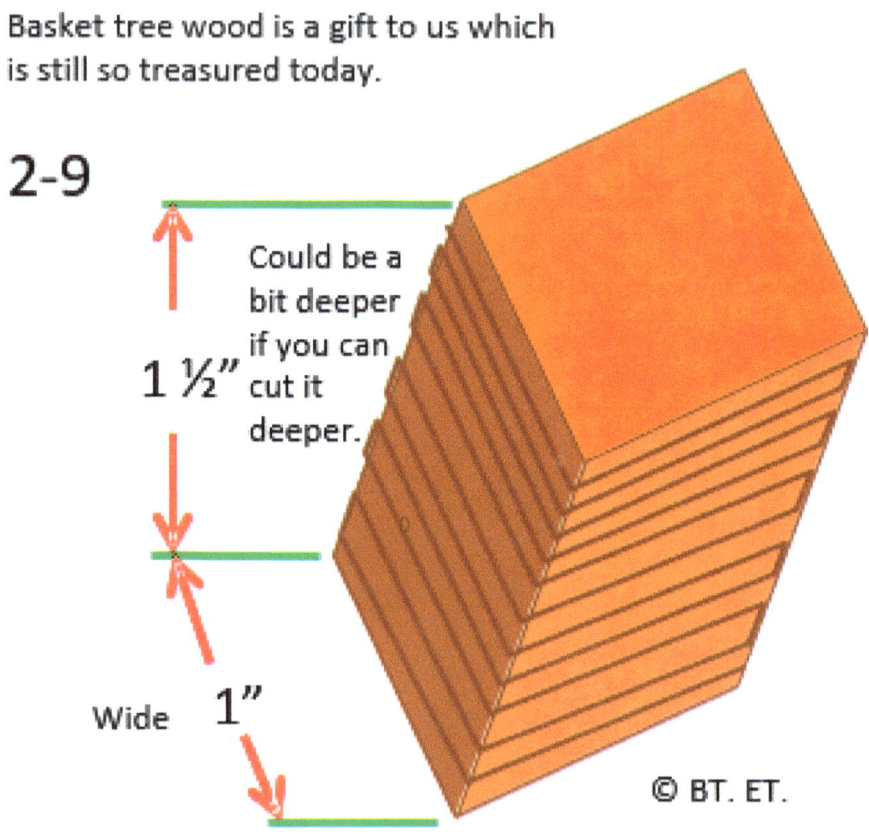

2-9

1 ½" Could be a bit deeper if you can cut it deeper.

Wide 1"

© BT. ET.

The glue between the years growth rings is not so strong when the tree is still green and the first few in inches of the sap wood is the best material. The pours or little holes are easily crushed or pounded or sharp bending will let the years grown come apart.. There are many way to accomplish this which you may even invent your own way. The key is to get the right tree to begging with.

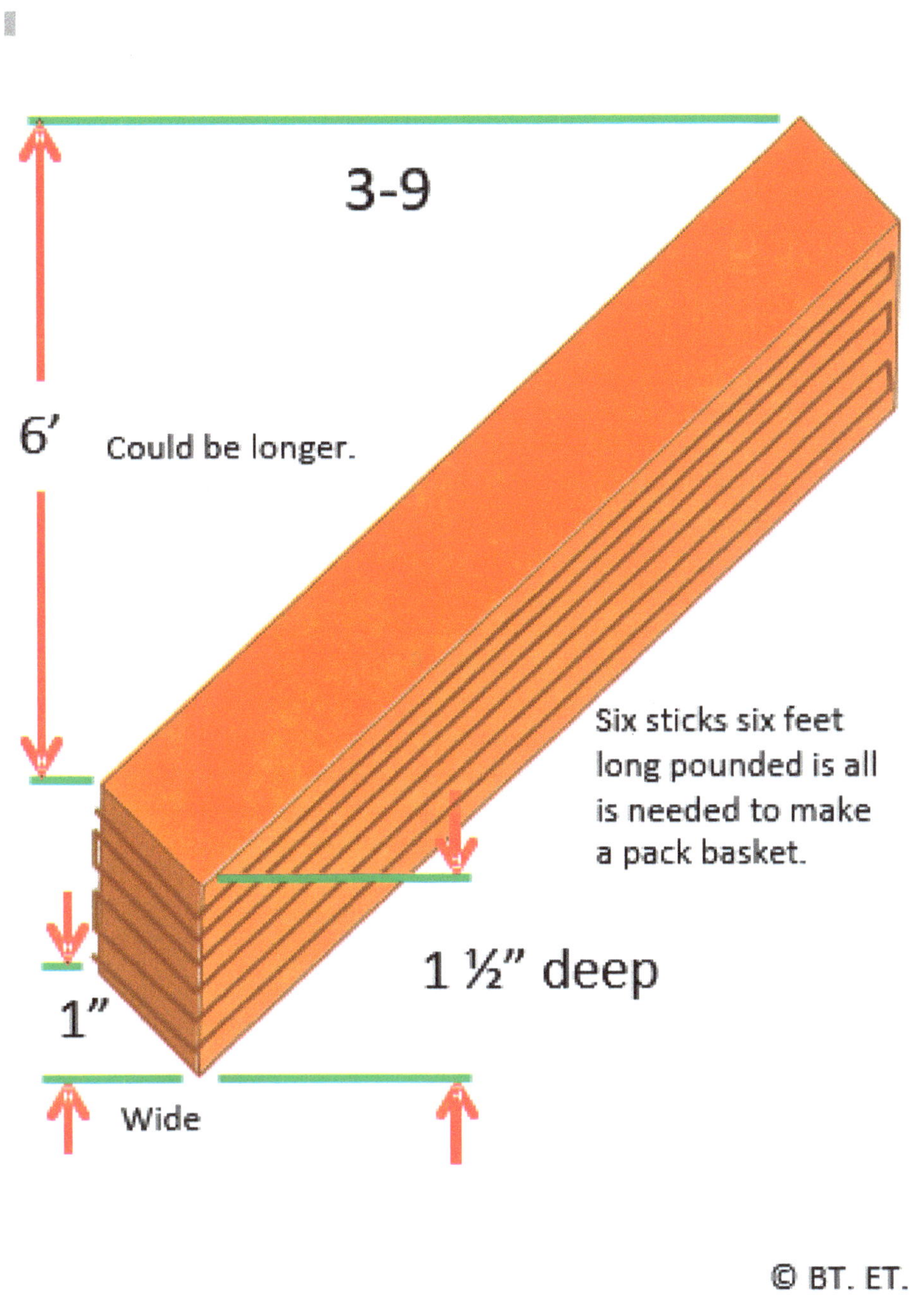

3-9

6' Could be longer.

1" Wide

1 ½" deep

Six sticks six feet long pounded is all is needed to make a pack basket.

© BT. ET.

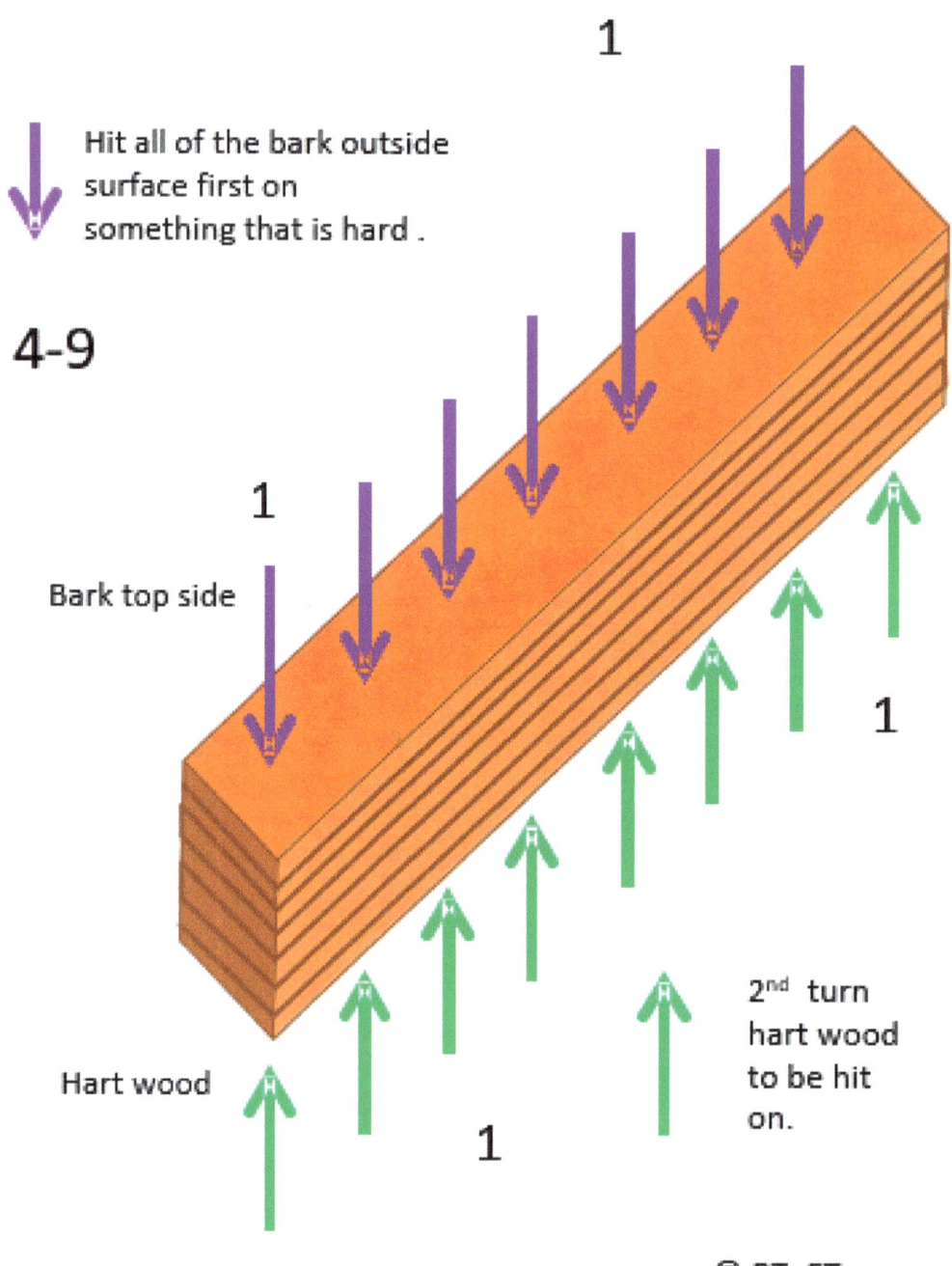

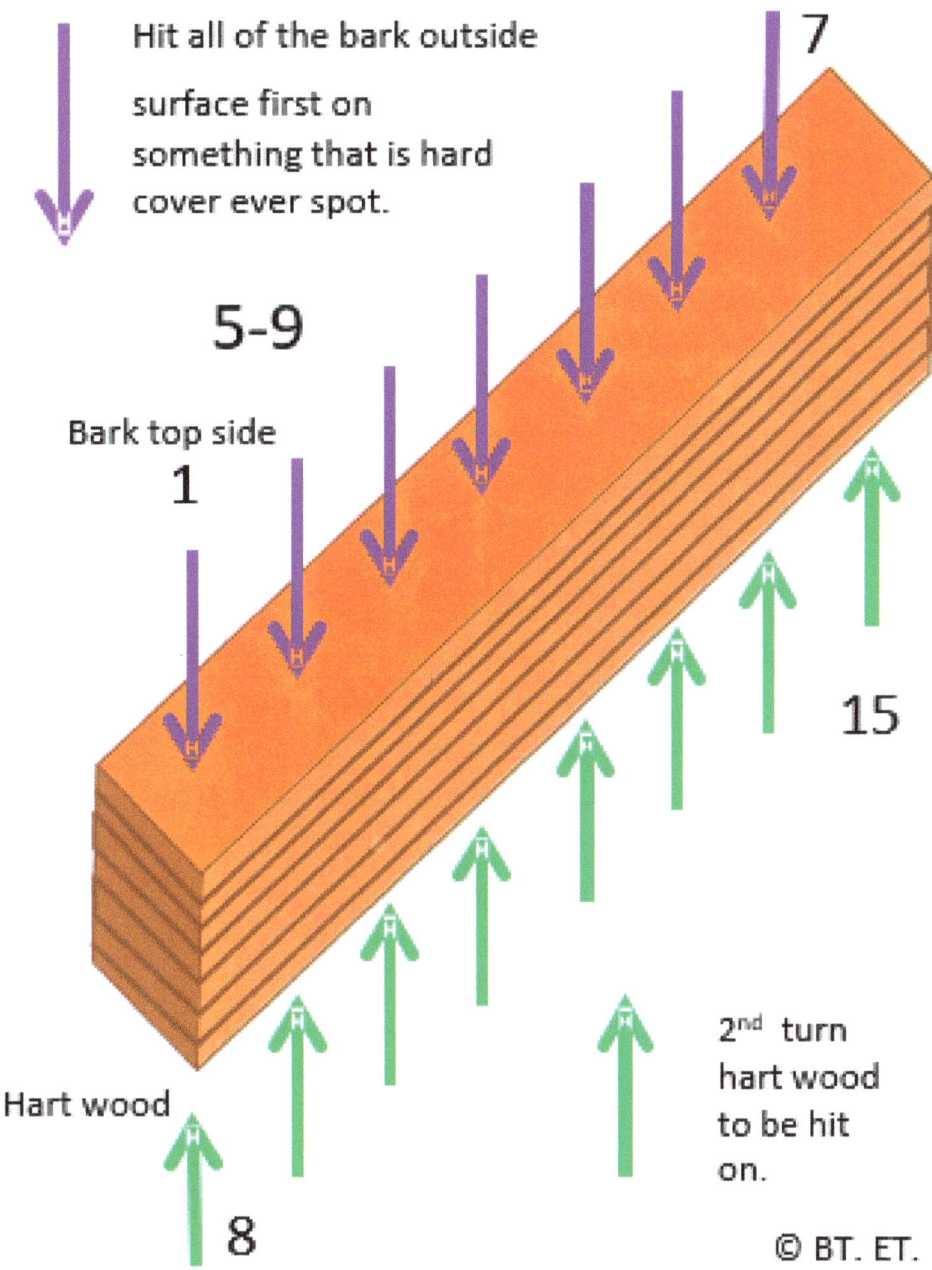

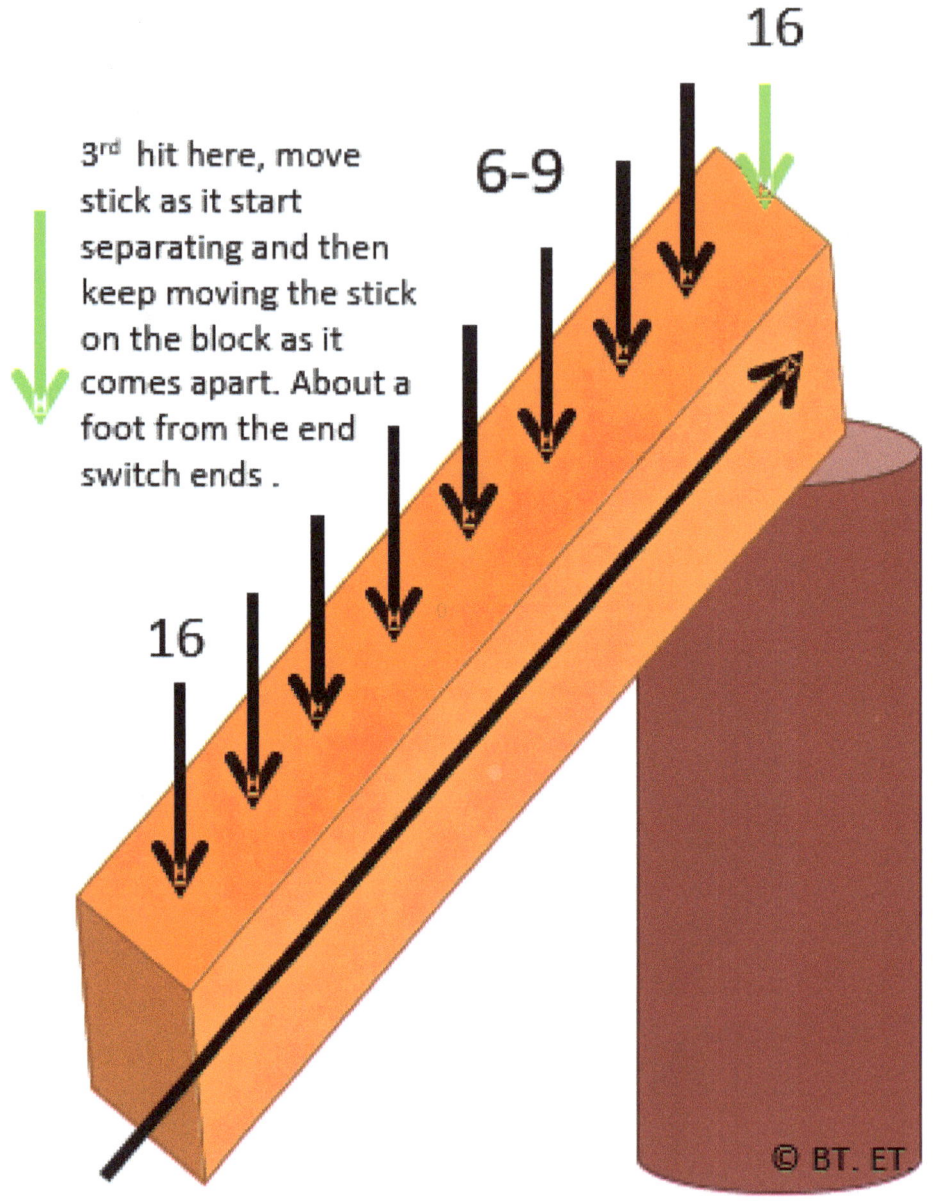

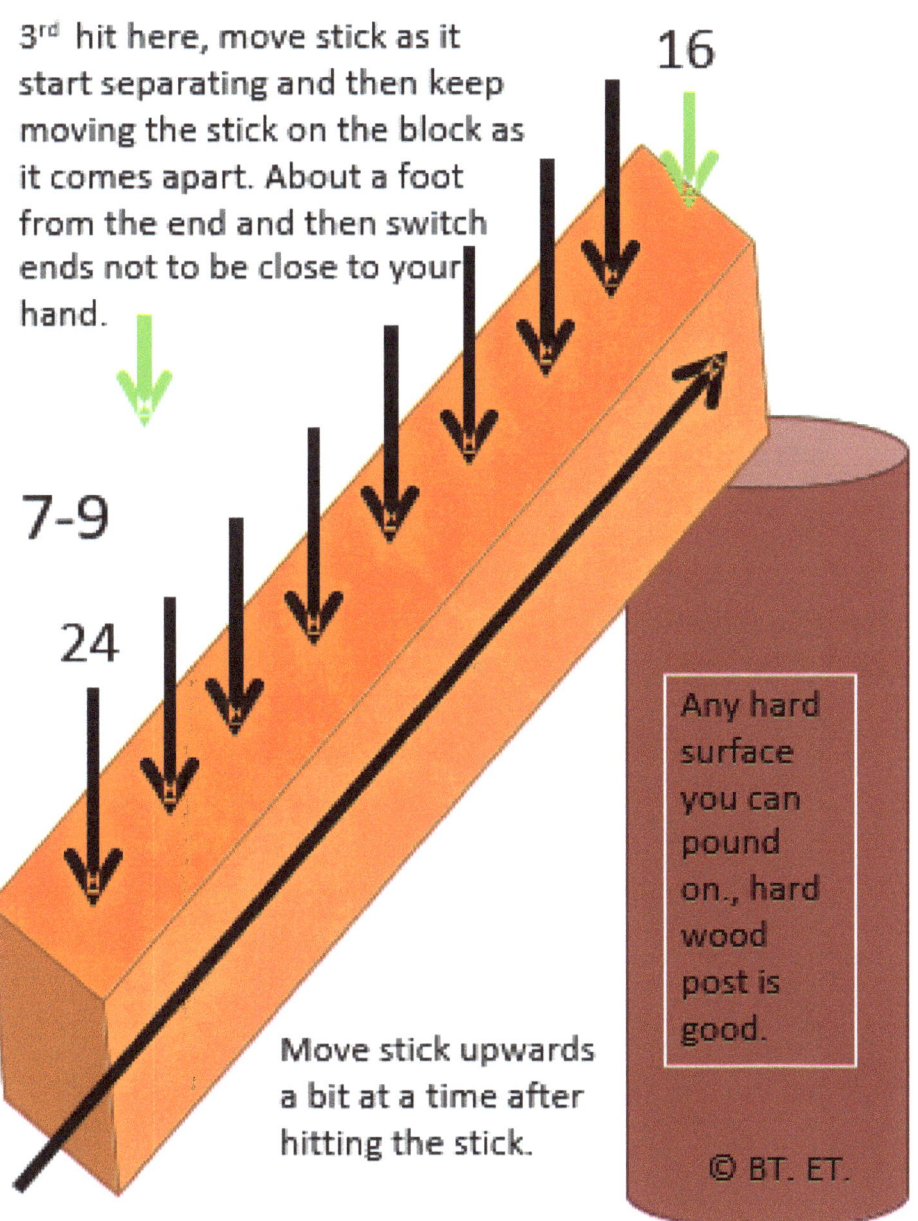

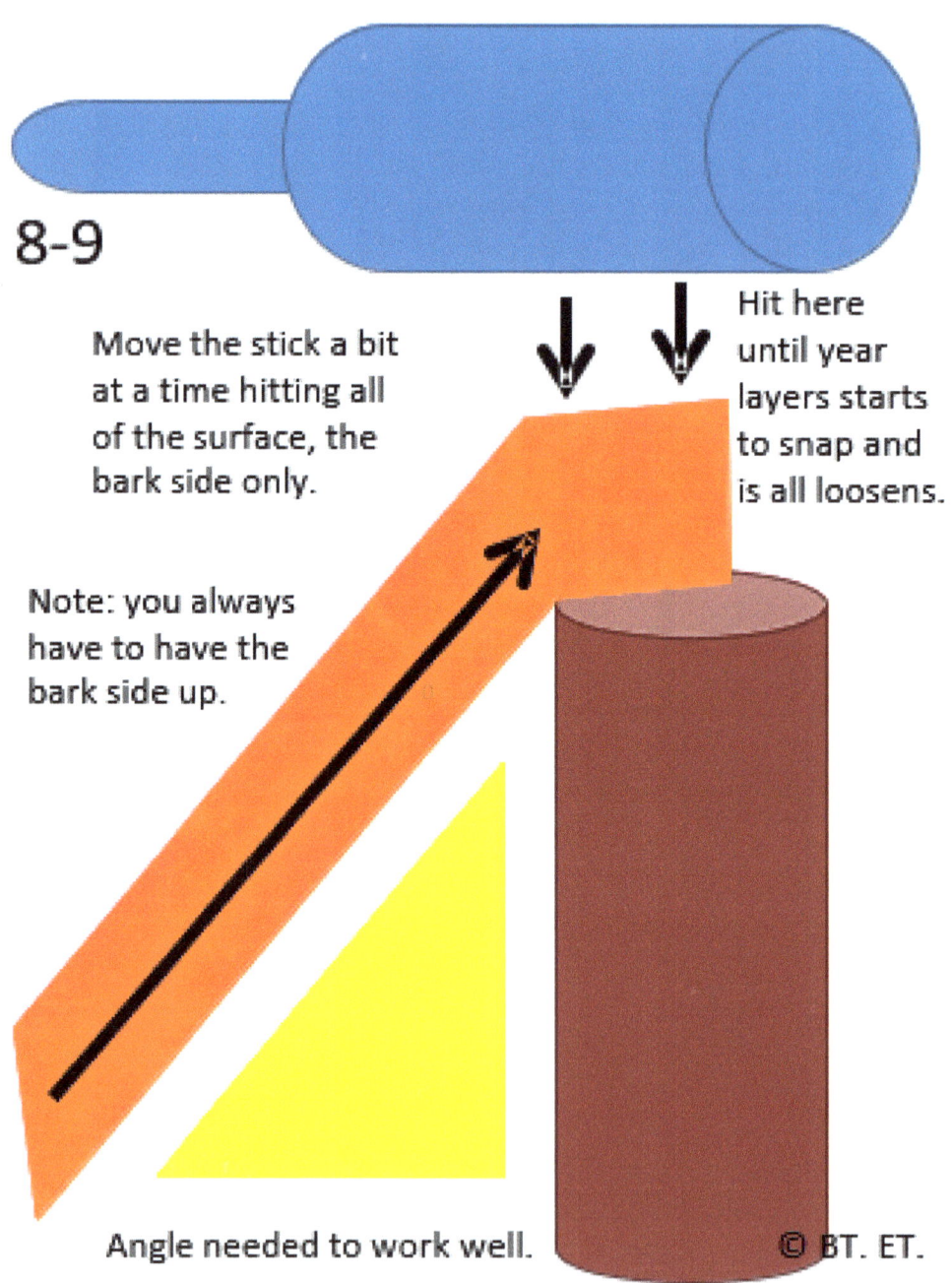

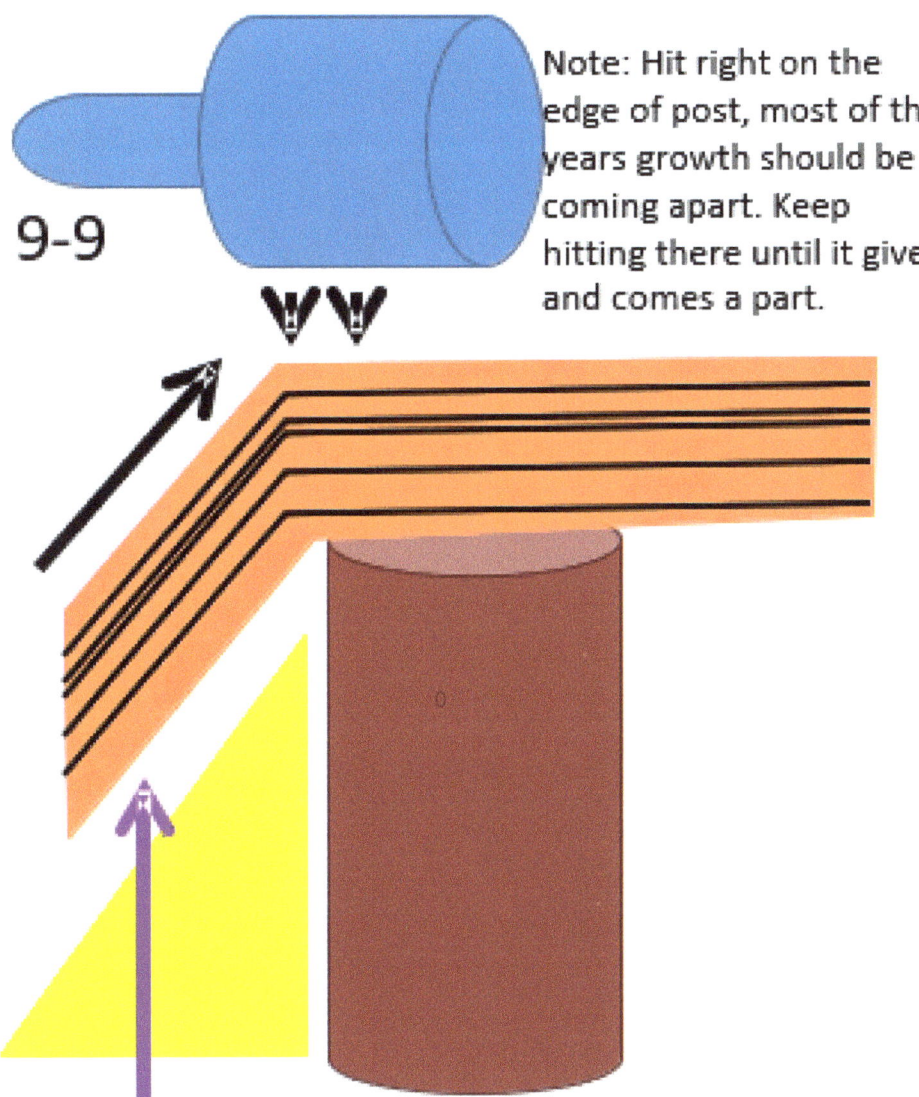

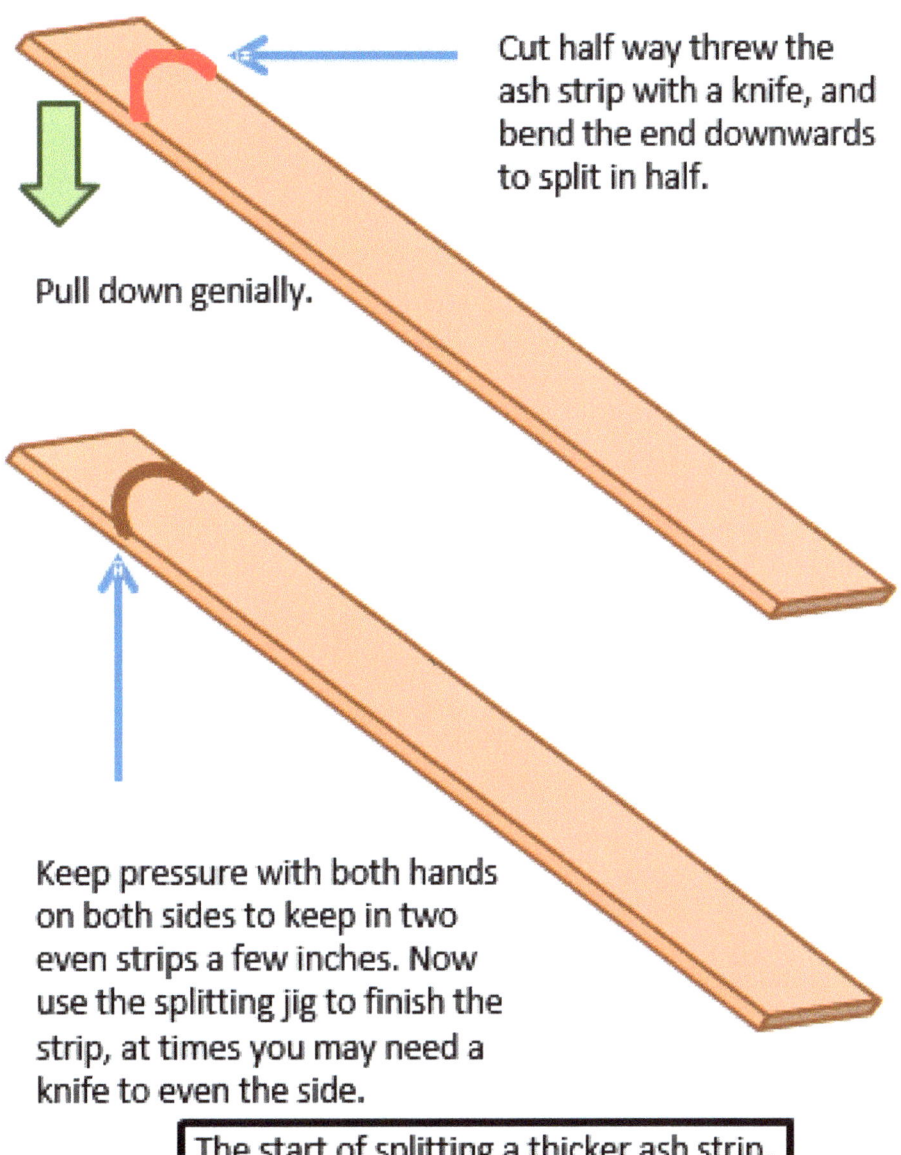

Cut half way threw the ash strip with a knife, and bend the end downwards to split in half.

Pull down genially.

Keep pressure with both hands on both sides to keep in two even strips a few inches. Now use the splitting jig to finish the strip, at times you may need a knife to even the side.

The start of splitting a thicker ash strip.

Notes:

• CHAPTER 7 •

Rawhide

Before the basket rims are ready to make, you will need to prepare your rawhide. Rawhide is made from a cow or bull skin. (Deer and moose are too stretchy. They are harder to cut, work with, and do not work well. Beaver rawhide may repel water, but it is not as strong as cowhide.) Cattle hides make the best rawhide because they are thick and can be pre-stretched before lacing. Then, there is no further stretching. As the weaving dries, the rawhide will pull the frame in very tight, which is very important for good working baskets.

GETTING A COW SKIN

The best time to look for a cow is in the fall, or early spring, when the skin has a good thickness and a better quality. Big animals in the summer are also good because they are not so thick. Big bull skins are not too good for rawhide because the skin is thick, and it weighs more. (Farmers, prior to electricity, would butcher their animals in early December when the snow brought the cold weather). Now, we can get hides just about any time, so we prepare the rawhide early in the spring or fall when there are fewer bugs and cooler weather. Hides can only be kept dried, salted, or frozen.

Most of time, you need to know what you are going to do with the skin of rawhide ahead of time. At least, try to save the thick part of the skin if you must take care of the skin quickly. There will always be a lot of small rawhide on the other skins that you get. On average, one cow skin will make enough rawhide to do many baskets.

The first place to look for cow skins is at farms in the area where you live that butcher their own stock. It is a good idea to have contact with various cow farmers ahead of time. This is the best way that I have found to purchase skins at a reasonable price from 15 to 30 dollars is a good price.

Several farmers may need to be contacted before you begin your project to see when the skins will become available. When getting a cow skin, both cow and bull are okay. Holstein types of cows are best that we have found. It is important to explain to the skinner of the rawhide that you prefer that the skins do not have cuts in them. Inspect the skin before making the final purchase. Even if it might cost extra for a good skin, it is worth it if it is free of too many cuts. To ensure that the skin will be unmarred, tell the skinner that it is okay to leave some fat or meat. The person skinning the hide needs to be careful and know your requirements beforehand.

The first place to look for cow skins is at farms in the area where you live that butcher their own stock. It is a good idea to have contact with various cow farmers ahead of time. This is the best way that I have found to purchase skins at a reasonable price from several farmers may need to be contacted before you begin your project to see when the skins will become available. When getting a cow skin, both cow and bull are okay. Holstein types of cows are best. It is important to explain to the skinner of the rawhide that you prefer that the skins do not have cuts in them. Inspect the skin before making the final purchase. Even if it might cost extra for a good skin, it is worth it if it is free of too many cuts. To ensure that the skin will be unmarred, tell the skinner that it is okay to leave some fat or meat. The person skinning the hide needs to be careful and know your requirements beforehand.

Occasionally one of these farmers may contact you when they have a dead cow and want to give it to you. Some years, when there is no market for hides, you can get hides for nothing, since they are throwing them away. We prefer working the fresh hide. Skin the cow immediately in the summer months and within a day or so in the winter months, if the cow skin is kept in a cold place.

If you must wait for some time before using the hide, fold the hide hair out and freeze it, and a bit of big salt on the flesh part of the skin. A freezer can be used to keep the rawhide frozen until it is needed. It may take a few minutes or so to thaw, depending on the temperature. It is always a good idea to get a few cow skins at a time, because doing a lot of skins ahead of time gives you a good supply to work with and to choose from for different baskets. Don't use rawhide if it is rotten the smell, the slime, and the way it looks and feels are indicators to watch for. When cutting and stretching, it will break and look bad.

Storing a Cow Skin

Salting is a way of preserving a cow skin for years if it is done right. No more than one year is best. (I would not keep the skin salted in the summertime if I can help it.) Open the cow skin flat with the hair side facing the ground. Then, using big salt grains spread the salt so that the skin is well covered on the flesh side. Salt is not expensive, so really be generous with it. Fold the skin onto the skin side, then the hair-on-hair and so on until you have a square looking pile of skin.

Now tie it up with string like a package. Storing skins this way makes them easier to move around. Try to place the salted skin in a dry place at a slight angle so that the juices can run out away from the skin. An old bathtub with a metal cover works well. Make the tub so it can drain, and animals cannot eat or spoil it. For the best result, do not keep it past the spring or warm weather.

When ready to use the cow skin, wash it to remove the salt before you start the process. Place the salted skin in a container of water for a day to get the salt and dirt out of the skin. Move the skin around in the water to help the process. Salted skins are a bit harder to take care of, so I would recommend that you use fresh skins if possible. Also, not having to salt the skin and remove the salt will save time.

Processing Skin - Needed Equipment

Fleshing a cow skin can be a very slow process, but it must be done. Tools needed: a square edge drawknife, a sharp drawknife, a utility knife, a pulley and rope, three or four 50-gallon plastic barrels, cold hardwood ashes, hydrated lime, a standing tree to hold the pulley and a J hook to move the skin up and down from one barrel to another barrel, a sander for the beam, a plastic apron, a big knife to cuts scraps, a sharpening stone, plastic pail for waste, a rain jacket, tall rubber boots, a hat, safety goggles, rubber gloves with grips on them, rags to wipe off your knife, access to water, a block-and-tackle on a bench to hang up the skin.

The block-and-tackle will make it easier to split the skin in half if it is too big, a stirring stick and a short rope about 6-foot for holding the skin from the center of the neck. One end of the rope should be left outside of the barrel and easy to find when lifting the skin. When most of the water has run off the skin, cut the skin in half while still hanging. Then place it on the fleshing beam to remove the hair first.

When using the fleshing knife, keep safety in mind because it can cut. I took a two-handed drawknife and straightened the handles with a torch and put on a slide stop block to stop my gloved hands from sliding onto the blade. I then bent it with the heat from a torch to round the blade a bit. Use the plastic apron, high rubber boots, safety goggles, and rubber gloves, to limit contact of solutions with your skin and to keep yourself dry and clean.

The fleshing beam can be made easily by taking a yellow birch log six feet long and splitting it in half. Remove the bark, drill two holes at a slight angle underneath, and place two peg legs into the holes toward the upward end of the beam. The beam, half a log, is placed at an angle of about 90 degrees or place to your hip for easy usage. Different legs for different heights will help better position the skin for working. A fleshing beam can also be purchased commercially. At times, sand or rub the fleshing beams to get the gashes out as they are made; I have made some accidental cuts on the beam at times. I always take a shower right after fleshing and wash my hands often!

SET-UP

Preparing the rawhide is one of the major steps. (In the old days, the hide would be nailed to walls and allowed to dry. Then it would be dried hard. A sharp, slightly rounded tool would be used to scratch the hair off. This process could take days, since only about a quarter of an inch could be scraped at a time in short strokes.) The fall time or on a cool spring day before the bugs come out is a good time to remove the hair and flesh off the skin. One a day can be done for a few days.

Working outside is best because it can smell a bit. After some time, you will not even smell it. That is why the skin must be done right away. Wind can also help with the smell. Select a place where good footing is guaranteed. Make sure your fleshing beam cannot move. Secure it to a piece of plywood to be sure. Because the process of removing hair and flesh from skins requires several sharp tools, it is very important to create and maintain a clean and safe workspace. Always have sure footing when moving the skins. Never be in a hurry to do anything; the extra time is worth your safety. Pay attention to what you are doing and try to complete the process before stopping because it is hard to start and stop.

PROCESSING THE HIDE

The fresh hide is placed in cold water to make sure it stays wet and clean. The hide must be completely wet to process in a solution of hydrated lime and hardwood ashes. When applying hydrated lime, watch for the dust. Use a mask. In a plastic 55-gallon barrel over half full of water, you add three gallons of hydrated lime and three gallons of hardwood ashes. Stir well before putting the hide in it. (The solution requires one pint of lime and one pint of ash for each gallon of water.) Mix enough solution so the barrel will be more than half full depending on the size of the hide. You must stir the hide with a wooden paddle four times per day for the solution to work well. It will be easier with more than enough solution. Don't make it strong enough to burn the skin.

Before placing the hide in the solution, cut a short slit at the center of the neck one-inch in. Use that slit to lift the hide out of the solution. In the slit, tie a six-foot light rope to help find where the slit is when the hide is in the solution. Keep the rope end outside the barrel. Stir the hide and solution to make sure every part of the hide is being treated. Cover the barrels so nothing can fall in.

If the weather is warm, the solution will work faster. After two days, start checking if the hair is coming off when it is stirred. With rubber gloves, pull the hair here and there to see if it will come off easily. If the weather is cool, it will take longer for the solution to work. The solution can be made stronger if needed.

Use a set of block-and-tackle if the hide is heavy to move it up and stir it back down. With your gloves, take a pinch to see how loose it is. On the third day, start checking on the back of the neck towards the shoulders where the hairs are harder to loosen. It is best to try several different places on the skin. This hair test gives an accurate picture of the progress of the process. As soon as the hairs start slipping out easily, it is time to take it out of the solution.

If it is not ready, drop it back into the barrel and wait another day. It can take from three to seven days for the solution to do its work. Again, please be safe in all you do, always have a first aid kit available and water to flush your eyes or wash your skin. Once the hair slips off easy with your fingers, the hide is ready to be de- haired. Since the thickness of the skin is not the same everywhere, split the hide crosswise while it is hanging, about halfway behind the shoulders, to keep the thicker backend together. The front end tends to be thinner and more elastic. Working on only half of the hide is easier. We have adjustable racks that one man can handle to stretch these two pieces to dry. Let the skin drip, overnight if needed, before putting it on the stretcher.

REMOVING HAIR

The cowhides need to have all the hair removed first. Placing the skin on a fleshing beam, we use a straight handle drawknife with a rounded metal, square edge blade to help remove the hair from the skin. The drawknife edge should be dull for removing hair. When removing the flesh and fat, something under the skin like hair, might make your blade dig into the skin. It does not matter with the hair side because the duller square edge is being used, and it will not cut the skin. I like to remove the hair in the center and then remove the rest clockwise until it is all done.

Push down on the hair with the square edge of the drawknife moving downward. Remove the hair as the lifted edge is pulled back, lightly rubbing the hair off. The hair stuck on the square edge should be removed. Rub with gloves in some of the deep spots that the drawknife cannot reach to remove all the hair. A flat scraper can help at times and can help remove hair. Also, there other tools can be tried. Take your time with this process; the more hair removed at this point, the less that will have to be removed just before making the rims.

FLESHING THE HIDE ON THE BEAM

Once the hairs are removed, turn the hide over on the beam. The sharp edge of the drawknife, 13 inches or longer with a curved blade is used for fleshing. It has handles on each side that are about 6 inches long. With this sharp flesher, we remove the tissue, flesh, and fat, leaving only the skin needed for basket rims. We try not to cut through the hide. We find that using short strokes with this flesher works better and is less likely to make cuts in the skin. A few sharp meats cutting knifes can also help remove and cut the unwanted skin around the outer edges. A J hook with a handle can be used to help move the skin on the wooded fleshing beam. Make holes on the outside edges to help with this task.

Fleshing is very hard work for the first skin, but the more skins you do, the easier it is. A very sharp fleshing knife is the key. Keep the fleshing knife sharp and sharpen the whole shining part of the blade, not just the tip. A watered stone is best. Keep sharpening it. Be careful with the big drawknife. I like doing a small amount at a time, maybe 18-inch strips because it is an easy reach and the weight on the blade handles will help cut through all the fat and meat to the skin.

We first use the big sharp drawknife on the flesh side, then the backend, dull, smaller draw shaver to get it cleaned to the skin. The saw side of the big draw shaver can be used to remove some of the flesh and meat if it is stuck hard to the skin, but I hardly use it. Use the drawer shaver in a sawing motion to remove the flesh off the skin. There are many approaches for using the drawknife to remove flesh from the skin. Experiment and find a process that works. Having a partner to help with the cleanup of the skin makes the process go much faster.

The back of the skin end is harder to do because sometimes the flesh is really stuck on. Cut off all the bad spots and pieces that stick out a bit on the skin and around the neck. Trimming around the neck, where the hide is too thick to work will help save money and time. Do not process skin that cannot be used. Again, ensure fleshing beam is secure.

Keep your back straight when fleshing and take breaks as needed. Wear high boots, an apron, safety glasses and plastic gloves.

Remember, the area around the skin will be slippery and wet: take time and be very careful when handling sharp tools.

The skin at this time is thick and swollen because the solution has caused the pores to open. The skin is then washed in cold water and placed in a solution of lactic acid (two ounces of lactic acid for every ten gallons of water) for twenty-four hours to prevent the skin from being damaged. The skin should be stirred in this solution at least four times in the 24 hours. Apple cider vinegar can be used if lactic acid is not available. It neutralizes the action. The skin is then washed in about 70-degree water. It is hung up to drain to make it lighter. This is done before placing on a square rack to dry. If you wanted to make leather, this would be the right time, since the pores are still open. A slight smell is okay. If it is too smelly and slimy, then it is probably rotten and not good to use.

Preparing your own skins is hard, somewhat smelly, and slippery work, but with a little practice, you'll soon be able to handle several skins in a day. Preparing your own skins will save you money and working with materials you helped prepare is an important part of being a traditional basket maker.

STRETCHING

Working on a large table or while still hanging makes cutting the skin in half easier than cutting it on the ground. The skin now can be preserved by stretching it on an adjustable rack made into a square with four pieces of spruce wood, 2 inches by 3 inches width and at least 5 1/2 feet width by 8 1/2 feet length, until it is dry. Poles can also be made into a square frame big enough to fit the half hide. The stretcher is made adjustable by drilling holes in the wood overlap a little bigger than the corner bolts. On the inside of the rack, fence staples are placed on the frame. The holes should be six inches apart all around on the three-inch side of the frame so when the piece of skin is placed inside of the rack on top of a table, it can be adjusted allowing for some stretch. As it dries, opening some slits may be needed to give some slack on the frame so it does not twist as much. (The frame can also be used to dry and stretch leather).

We make our S-hooks to hold the skin with two- and half-inch nails (6-penny nails). The uses of regular nails are best because the rust holds the skin better. We make the hooks by using two five-inch spikes in a vise with the points sticking up above the vise about one inch. They are just far enough apart to pass a two- and half-inch nail in between them. With a large pair of pliers, we take a nail by the pointed end and place the head of the nail in between the spike ends and go around one of the ends creating a loop. Lift the loop and place it on the far point of the spike and turn the nail around the second end of the spike finishing the hook.

Use four 1/8-inch braided rope to thread through the staples on the rack, on each side of the wood of the rack. Leave about 3 feet of extra braided rope. Pliers can then be used to close in the end of the S-hook between the staples so that it does not come off the rope. The hooks that hold the hide can slide on the rope around the frame to tighten the skin. Place the S-hook point downwards to hold the skin. Place an extra hook at the end of the two fence staples. Use that last hook to help hold the rope tight. Just run the hook back and hold on one of the ropes that are holding the skin.

Start (1) On the center of the straight cut side of the skin, on the eight-and-a-half-foot estimate side of the rack. Run a strong, nylon braided line from the center fence staple, working through the skin hooks and fence staples toward the right. (2) Tie off the slack end from the last staple on an extra hook on the skin or on an extra staple. Do the same moving left from the straight edge. (3) To the end of the pole.

(4) Continue with the staple and hook combination on the opposite side (5) starting from one end ending on the other. Repeat on the last two sides (6 and 7). Once the skin is hooked in the rack, it is easy to tighten or loosen. Your hooks should point in the same direction. This method is efficient, centering the skin on the rack and limiting the waste.

A pointed knife is best to make the slot in the skin edges. Keep this knife sharp. The slot that you will make should only be a bit bigger than the nail. Make your slots about 1/8 inch from the edge of the skin so that you do not waste the rawhide.

It will take from a few days to a week to dry the stretched skin depending on heat and air humidity. Do not put in direct sunlight or where it is too hot. A fan may also be used to speed up the drying process of the skin. You will want to give the skin some slack as it is tightening. Even if the skin is not completely dry, you still may take it off the stretcher as long as it is fairly stiff. It will finish drying in time.

Once dried, the skin can be taken off the stretcher, rolled, and tied. It can be used whenever it is needed. Make sure you store it in a dry place where animals cannot get to it. Cut the skin crosswise in half to keep the thicker back together and the thinner shoulder and thicker neck section together. This is only done when a whole skin is ready to cut up. Cut it into strips for weaving any time by soaking the rolled skin in a barrel of water until you can find the soft and thin sections. This can be found on the belly sections of the skin. The underside belly of the animal softens first because it is thinner. Remove and save these pieces to cut later. You cut around the pieces.

CUTTING

The French word for cut rawhide strips is 'babiche'. A good piece of rawhide is needed to give the basket a better appearance. If there is a defect, it can be cut off or marked to later remove while cutting. Do not try to cut too big a piece of rawhide because it will take a longer time to cut, and it will be more difficult to maneuver. It will also have more stretchy parts throughout the piece that needs to be considered and cut out. Remove the outer skin holes first. Cut along the outer edge going around the whole piece, cutting corners as they become sharp corners.

Thin pieces of rawhide should be used right after it is cut. If not, freeze in the snow in a plastic bag or dry it until needed. If it is frozen, put it in water for about an hour or so, keeping an eye on it for use when it is ready. Just let it thaw out a bit at a time, while checking it periodically. Dried rawhide can be put in water to soak overnight. The thickness of the rawhide is an important factor for deciding how long to let it soak. Repeated thawing helps determine needed time for different widths and sizes.

Rawhide Cutting Table w/Heavy Wheel - When cutting, we clamp a five-inch-long, one-and three-quarter inch block of wood with a half inch slot at one end with a slit made, with a hack saw, to insert a utility blade. We made marks on the block next to the blade to show how wide we are cutting. Once we have cut two or three feet of rawhide by hand, we anchor the end to a shaft that has a heavy three-foot diameter wheel that pulls the raw hide when it turns. The weight of the wheel creates a steady tension that cuts smoothly as the wheel is turned. With the right hand, we turn the wheel and with the left hand, we guide the width of the rawhide on a table in a continual circle. We can start and stop instantly. The cutting with this wheel also helps stretching and even narrowing the width when cutting. The utility knife is a sharp tool with an exposed blade that can be used to cut the square corners off the pieces and to help trim off the bad spots. Once, every three or four skins, or when the pulling gets too hard, change blades in your cutter.

Small Rawhide Cutting Tool (Rawhide Sizing Holes w/3 Hole Craft Blade): When cutting the thin smaller rawhide, you drill a hole the same size you want on the edge of a block of maple, clamped to the table. Screw in a small blade that will form a part of the hole that the rawhide will pass through. Cut a narrow strip a few inches long using the utility knife, then use pliers to pull it through the hole with the blade until you are sizing it, and cutting it at the same time. This rawhide is ready to be used.

After you have finish cutting the hide into wide or thin webbing, you roll it loosely so it can dry to be used whenever needed. Cut the skin into strips for weaving any time by soaking the rolled hide in a barrel of water until the heaviest part of the skin has softened, making it easier to find the thinner sections that are usually on the belly. The thicker and stronger part of the skin will be cut three eight to half inch wide by cutting around the piece.

It will be easier to cut the thicker and stronger part into strips if the skin is somewhat still stiff. Depending on the thickness of the skin, cut the strip between 3/8 inch and ¼ inch wide, by cutting around the piece. Going around, keep rounding the sharp corners with a can reach the shaft with the wheel. The rawhide you are using can have different thickness and stretchiness, so by forcing it through the blade and hole, you are stretching it while keeping the hole full. The small thick pieces with all the bends can be used for wrapping top/back ends of the snowshoe frames. Sharp turns are weaker keep that in mind or do not use. The long strip of rawhide can be rolled loosely on the rack or spools for faster rolling and removal and keeping dry. It will also be easier to keep dry when used later as needed. Date the skin with a pencil when it when finished rolled and tied up. Place skin roll in a dry place where it will be safe from animals and moisture.

At first do not try to cut a piece bigger than you can handle, maybe two feet by two feet round. Feel the thickness with your hands as you turn it while cutting. A round piece of rawhide is easier to handle and to cut, but you tend to have more waste. Odd shapes are fine once you know how to trim corns as you cut. When you come to holes or cuts in the hide, cut them off just before you get there and keep going. Always have the flesh side of the hide upwards so it will be easier to see the cuts and defects as you come to them and remove as needed, so you have good rawhide.

To cut smaller strips for weaving baskets, use the pieces of thin skins of different thickness and stretchiness. Use only about 18 inches by 18-inch pieces of thin rawhide at first and a skin with the same thickness throughout to make it easier. Soak the pieces of skin until fully soft, and then start by cutting a strip with the right size.

A tester can be made in a piece of wood with a hole and a V slot taken out of the wood. Place it in the V slot to see if it fits snug in the hole. Once the rawhide is dry for a few minutes it will shrink. Also, keep in mind that the hole on the frame is one size bigger. If the rawhide breaks after the hole, change the blade or cut a bit off the piece of rawhide at the hole. You may come across places that just break for unknown reasons. Do not be concerned with those pieces, just get rid of them. Twisting rawhide while weaving makes the small rawhide stronger, like yarn, and makes it look better and more balanced.

Keep the similar rawhides together. Do not leave rawhide wet or moist too long because it will smell and start to deteriorate. A cap full of tide detergent in five gallons of water can help reduce the smell of the rawhide before using it. You will soon find out how soft you like it when cutting the rawhide. Hold the skin upward with one hand while cutting on the piece as the other hand turns the wheel. The wheel is big and heavy, pulling the rawhide down with a lot of power. If the skin is extra thin at places, it is no good for webbing the ends. Once it has been passed through the sizing hole, keep checking every 20 inches or so, that it is You want the small rawhide to fit

CARING FOR RAWHIDE

When rawhide is dry, it will keep for a long time. Rawhide can be wet and dry many times. When it is needed, let it soak in water. You can let it dry, and the process then starts all over again when you soak it overnight. The thicker the rawhide, the longer you will need to keep it in the water to get it soft before using. As rawhide dries, it tightens to give it more strength. Cutting your own rawhide into strips is the best because you can control for quality.

TIPS

When weaving the rims, do not pull too tight because it will not look right once they are done. The rawhide tightens as it dries. 2. Do not weave dry rawhide. It is hard on the hands and will not stretch or twist very well. Wet the rawhide as needed so it is workable. 3. Change the water often so that it does not go stale (smells). 4. Burning the hair off is a big mistake because the rawhide will lose its strength and you may not know it until the rawhide is put under pressure. It burns the woven strands within the skin and makes it weaker. 5. The sizing hole should be checked for hair and skin; it should be kept clean. If this is not done, it will change the size of the rawhide. 6. Put all your tools away once done and clean all your tools so rust does not get to it. A light oil rag helps on the metal tools. Also clean the mess. You do not need other things to happen or animal to get into this.

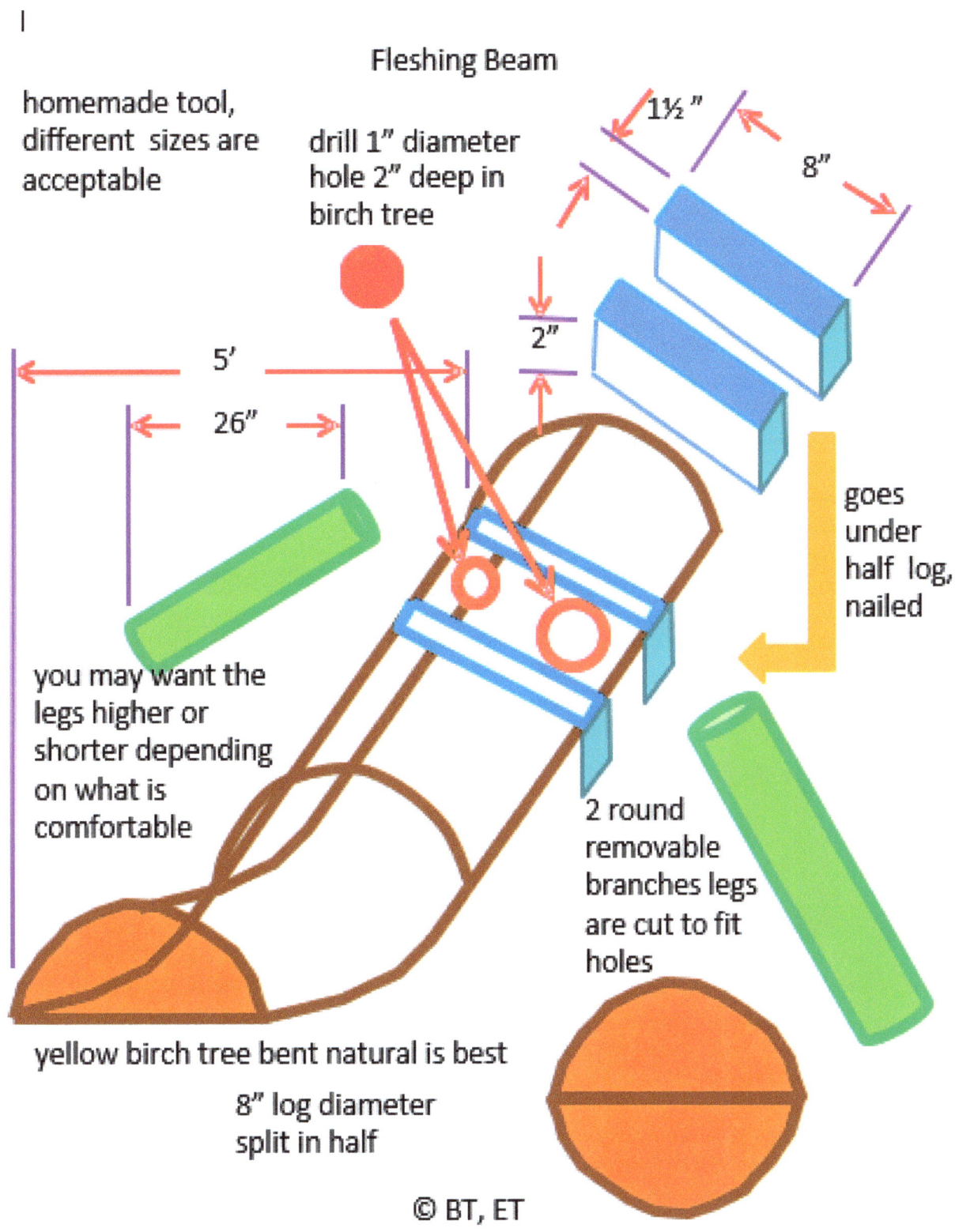

Center Rawhide Hardwood Cutting Tool
-see on page 3 of 3

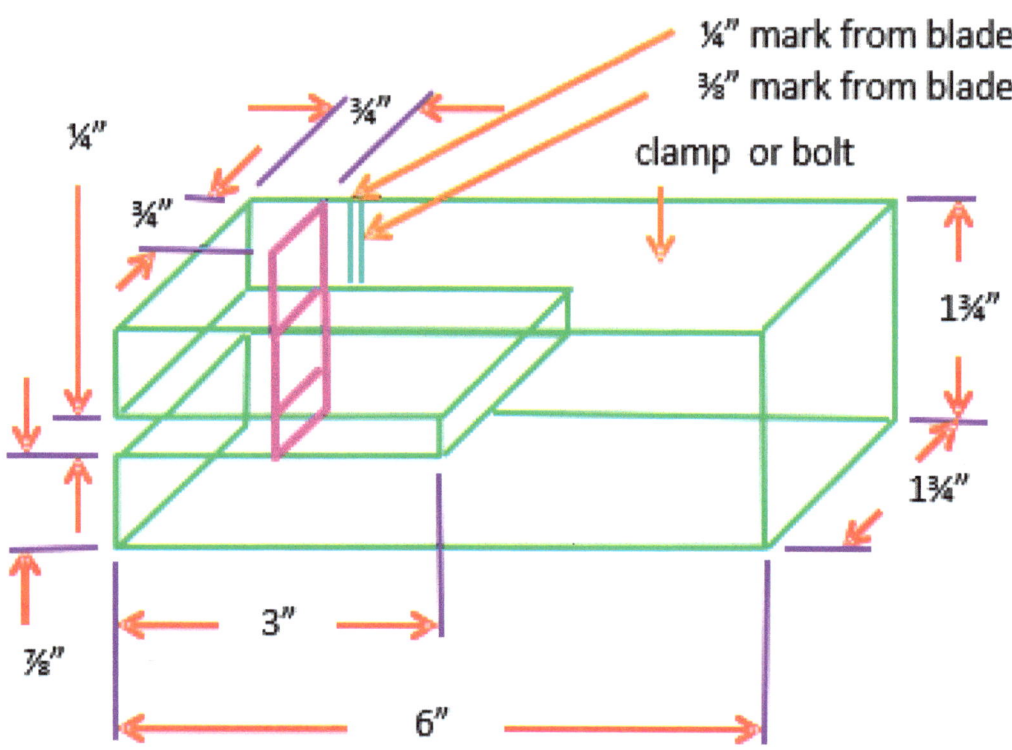

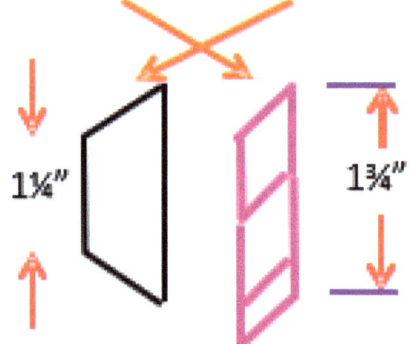

hacksaw cut for unity blade to be placed in tight and flush with wood

snap off extra part of blade that is extended above wood

© BT, ET

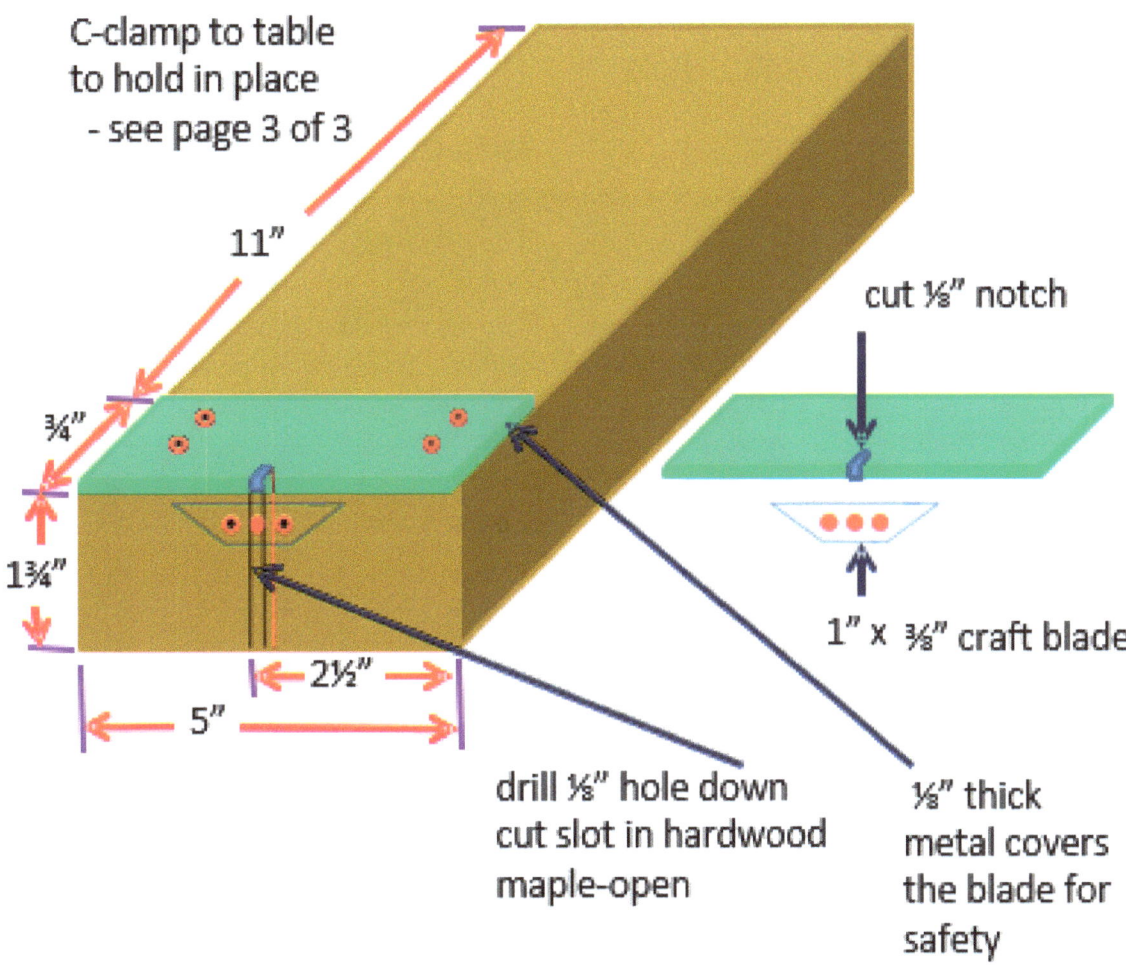

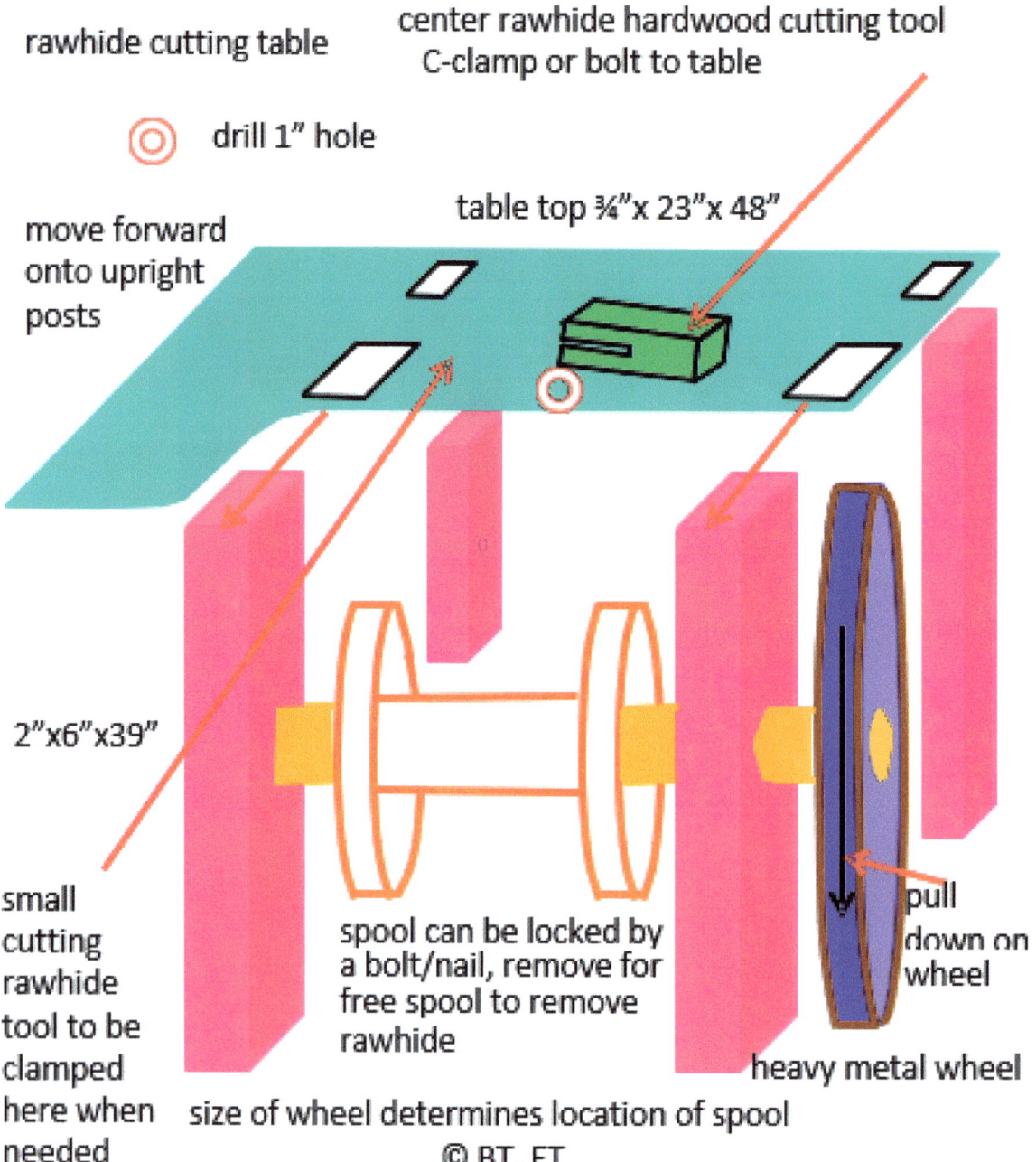

Rawhide Splice

this works for any size strips of rawhide for 100 % strength

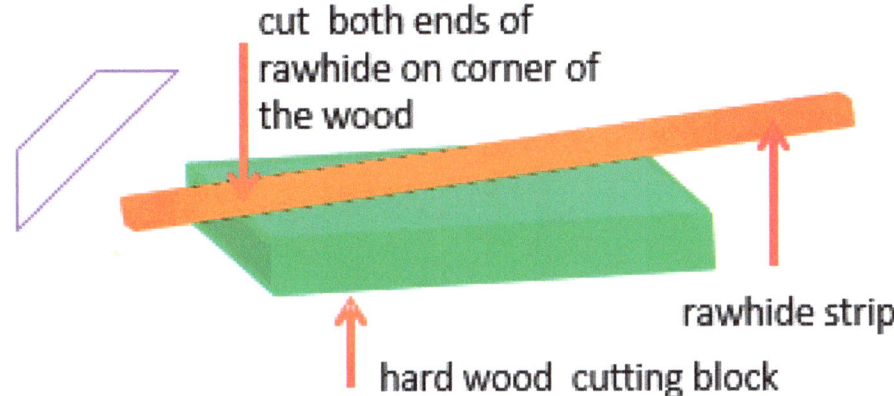

cut both ends of rawhide on corner of the wood

rawhide strip

hard wood cutting block

flatten rawhide with pliers if needed before cutting slot

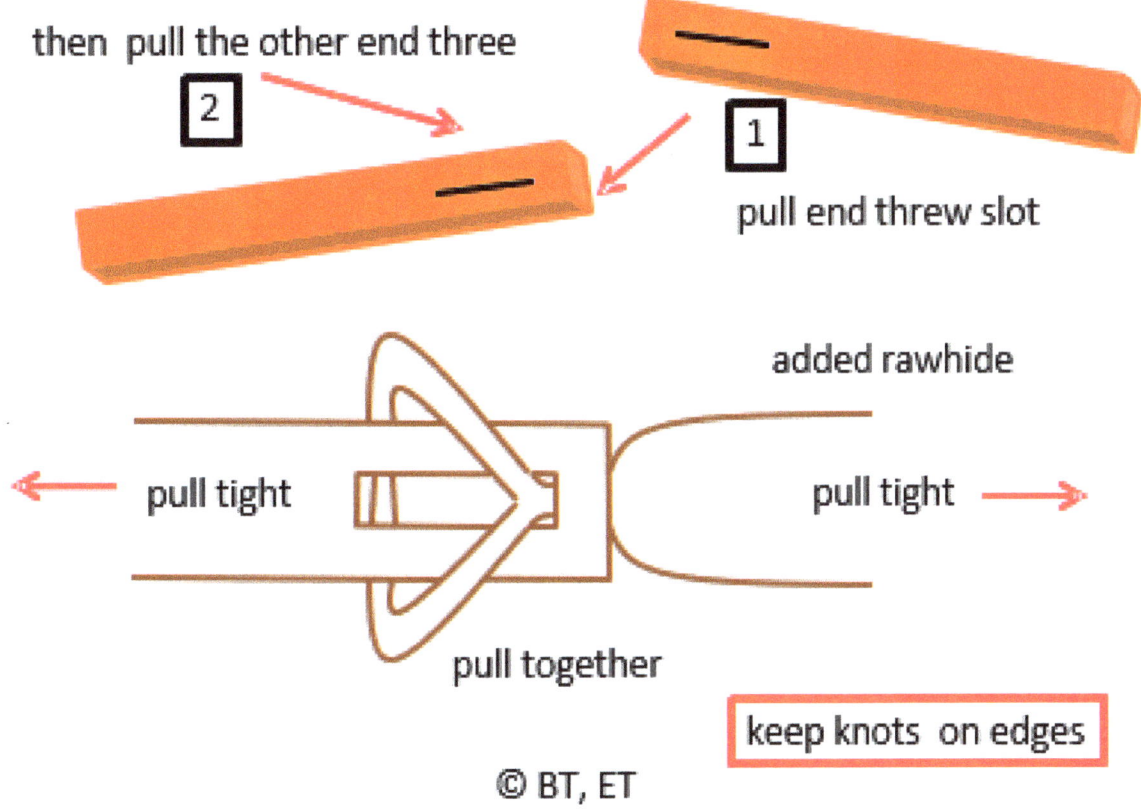

then pull the other end three

2

1

pull end threw slot

added rawhide

pull tight ← → pull tight

pull together

keep knots on edges

© BT, ET

Center Rawhide Stretcher Round Log Block

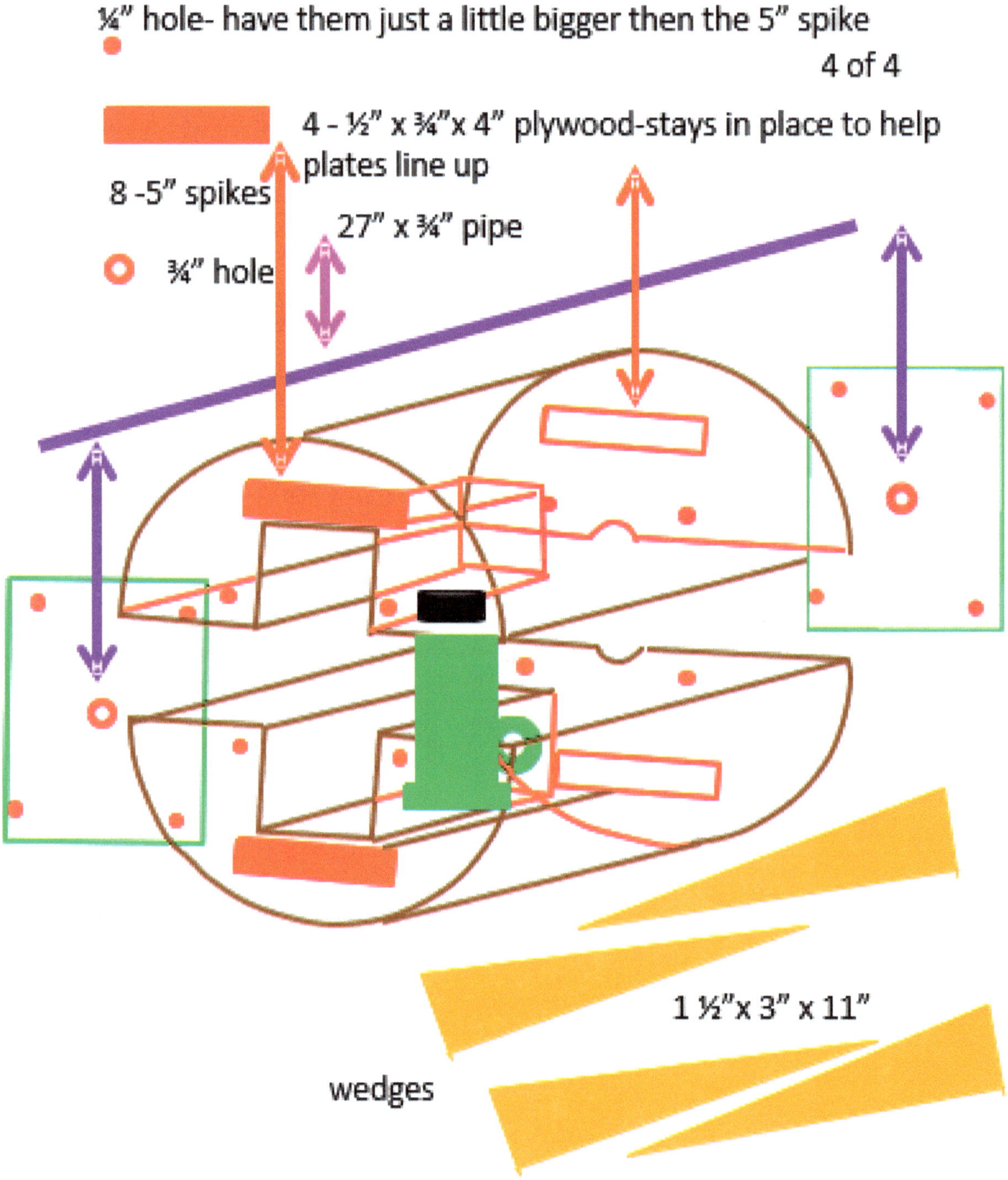

¼" hole- have them just a little bigger then the 5" spike

4 of 4

4 - ½" x ¾"x 4" plywood-stays in place to help plates line up

8 -5" spikes

27" x ¾" pipe

¾" hole

1 ½"x 3" x 11" wedges

© BT, ET

Center Rawhide Stretcher Round Log Block

- ¼" hole -- have them just a little bigger then the 5" spike
- 4 - ½" x ¾" x 4" plywood -- stays in place to help plates line up
- ¾" hole

27" x ¾" pipe

8 - 5" spikes, place in holes

put removable plates on block in place and then drill all holes

2 ton jack

© BT, ET

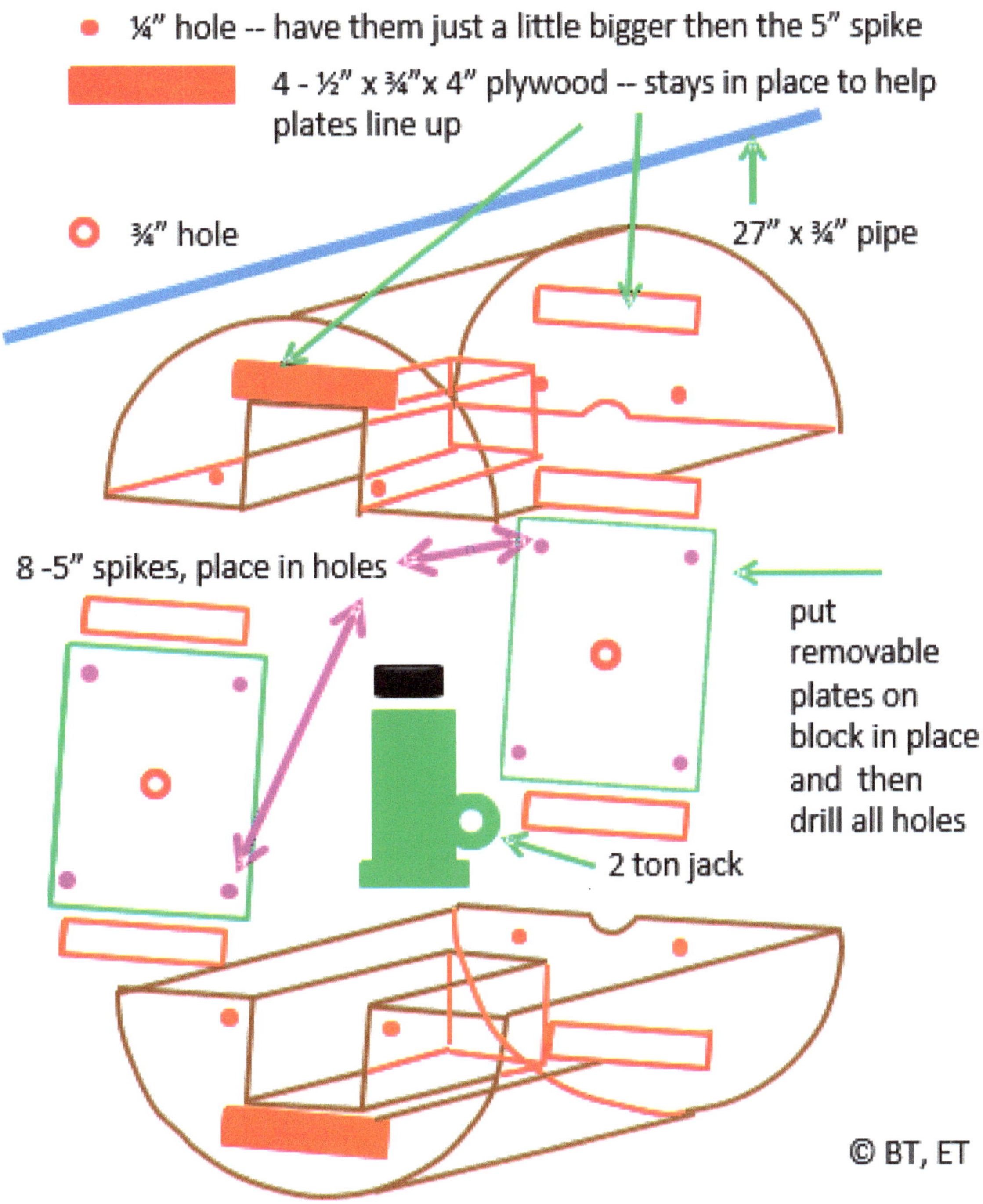

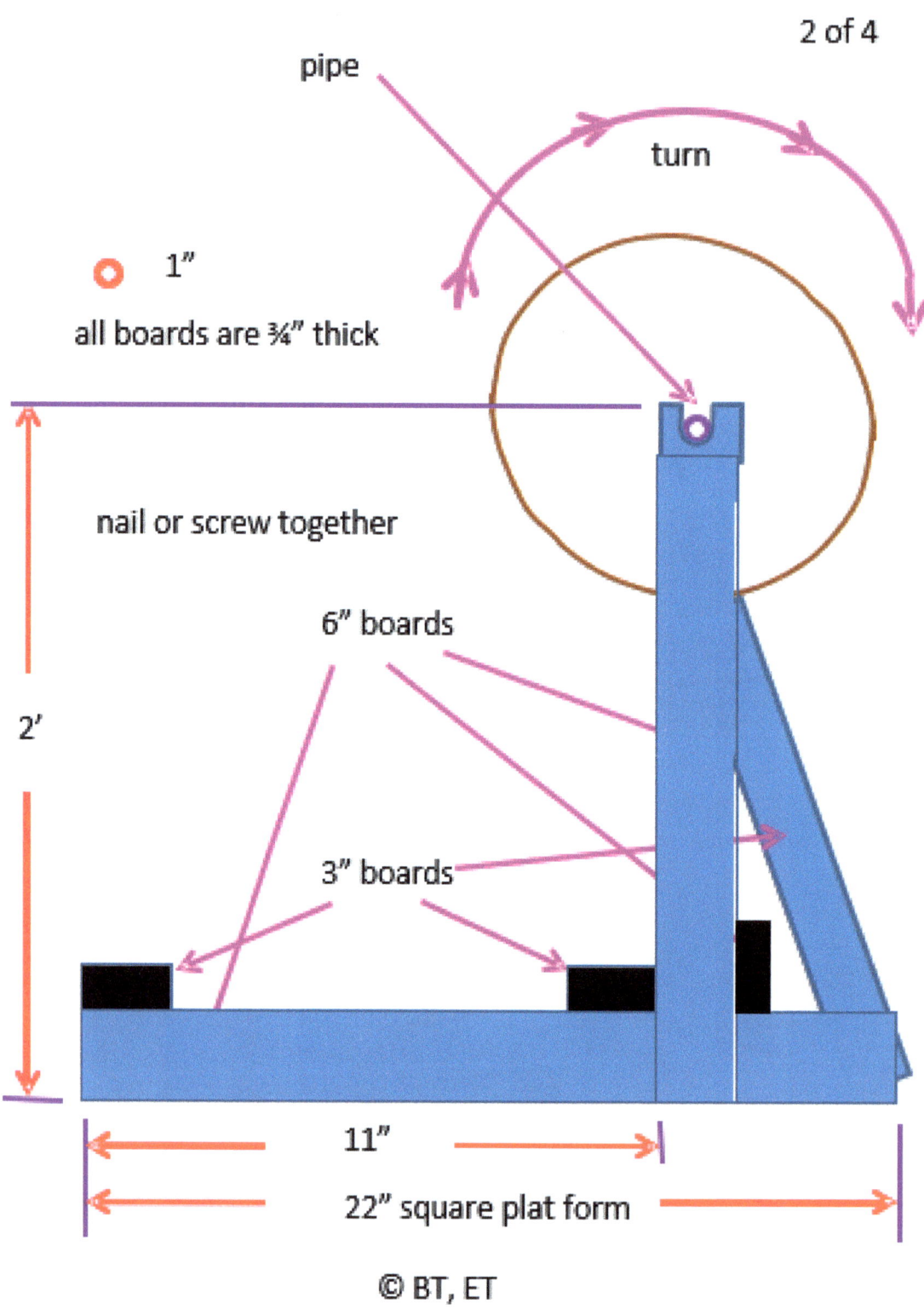

Center Rawhide Stretcher

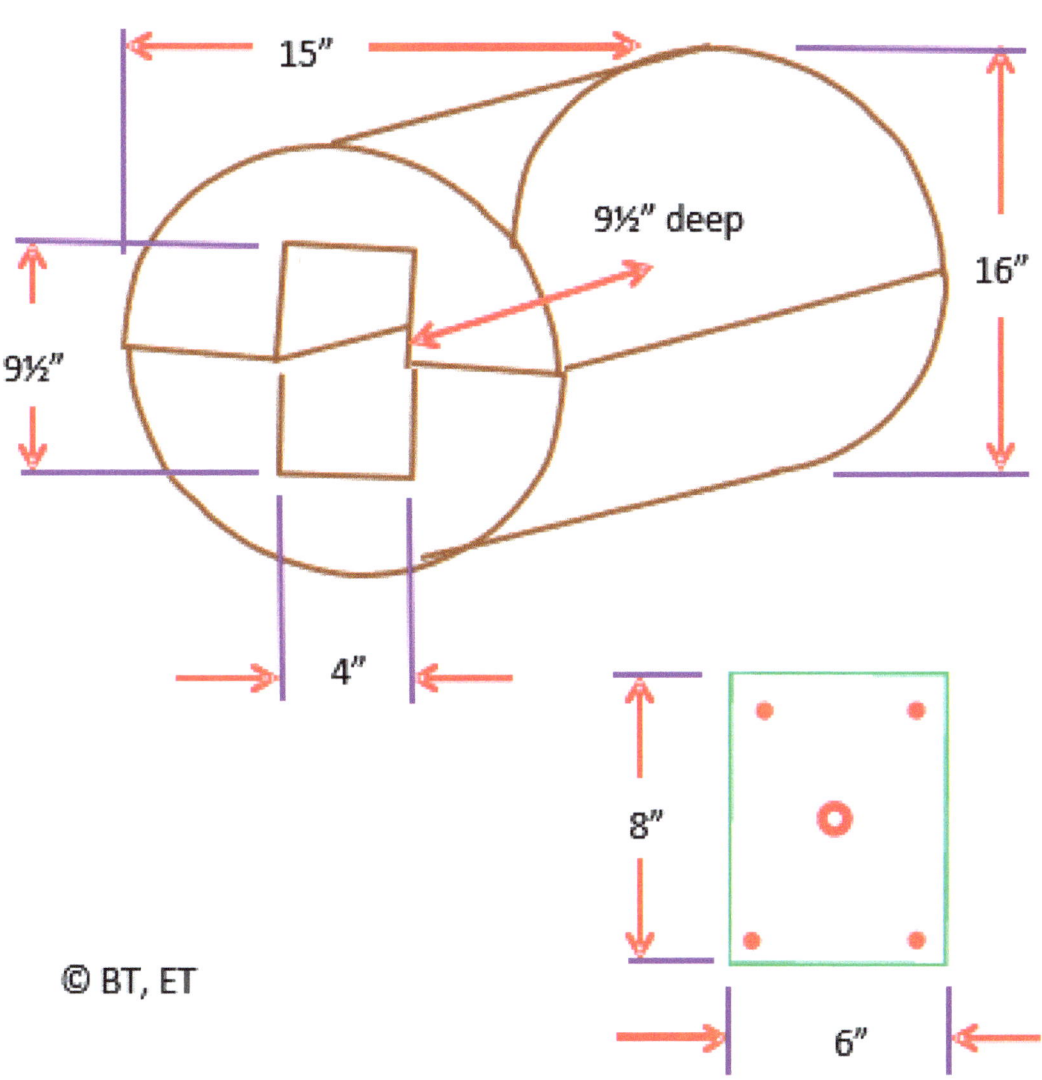

• CHAPTER 8 •

BASKET WEAVING

PREPARING WITH A PLAN

Note: Planning the basket is best way to make a great basket.

　　Pick the way you want to weave the basket. Pick the rims and handles ahead of time to make it easier. You want to split, cut, or scrap strips at this time if you can once you want to make a basket is now the best time. Dried and rewet to use can also be used at this time.

BASKET MOLD FRAMES

1. Molds are easy to make or try free hand.

2. Our molds (cage molds) are easy to use and light weight to move around.

3. Different heights and shapes of baskets what do you want?

4. It is easy to flatten the bottom of the basket because of the hollow indention of the mold.

5. Keeps the uprights lined up with the wood strips of the mold.

6. Marks on the mold (wood strips) lets you keep top of basket even as you go around weaving.

7. Rubber band keeps uprights in place and easy to move as needed.

8. Easy weaving with spaces on the mold frames up right wood strips which let you grip the weaver easily with the mold upright spacing.

9. Clamps can be used to hold uprights on the upward mold frame.

10. Leave on mold for easy and fast drying to keep the basket weave tight.

11. WEIGHT CAN BE ADDED INSIDE FOR FLATTER BOTTOM OF BASKET.

You can use the shape of jars, boxes, or containers as a mold and weave around it for its shape. Just keep in mind that when you're done most of the basket, you will need to take your mold out before finishing the basket.

MOLDS

NOTE: Basket should be made on a form or mold if you want them all the same. If the bottom of the basket is larger at the bottom than at the top, you will need a form that you can take out from the top opening. That is why a lot of shapes are at a slight outward angle to enable removal of the basket from the mold.

FREE HAND MOLD

Free hand is the best way to learn but takes more time to start. You need a higher skill level to make better baskets. (No mold, just knowing the size and shape wanted).

TAKE DOWN MOLD

Molds that are carved out of a single piece of wood will allow you to make baskets of similar sizes. Usually, several steps are taken in order to flatten out the bottom of the basket. Heavy weights can be placed on the round molds to keep the bottom flat while weaving. An available spray bottle of water is useful to keep your weaving moist and supple when weaving, (do not over water weavers and or uprights).

Some basket makers will just make their baskets in two or three steps. It is best to weave three or four rows and let dry overnight. The next morning re-tighten what you have woven and add three or four more additional rows. Repeat each day until you are at the top. At this point it is best to wait and let it set another day before bending it to form the top.

Pack basket mold

Molds can be made with cedar wood or any soft wood to put together so they can be taken apart once the basket is dried and the rims are ready to be added on. The size of the mold would depend on the size of the basket you want. The basket can be round bottom or flat bottom, and you can leave a knob on the top to use as a handle. Many old molds are still used today in a traditional way. Cardboard of the weaving pattern to start the bottom of the basket makes it easier to start. For our cardboard for the big pack basket is 7" wide and 9" long and is laid down with the four corners are black squares. Which once you lay the bottom weaver on the cardboard the four outside corners will be on top so that once you flip it over they will be your outside bottom corners. You will have 7 bottom upright pieces on the width with a space in-between and 9 bottom upright pieces on the long side. Six feet is all you need for the length of these pack basket uprights. If they are too long you can cut them, or just wait once you are close to the top of the basket then cut them where they make your height.

1. 6' long upright, which includes the bottom and total basket height.
2. 16 pieces of 1" or 7/8" wide uprights, 7 one side and 9 the other side weaved for bottom.
3. Once bottom is weaved and balanced the uprights and empty spaces, it is now ready to put on the mold. (Outside of the tree on the outside of the basket if you can for the look of the basket)

4. Once the finished bottom is on the mold, put the board screwed down on the bottom to hold in place. (Always work with the mold bottom upwards but can be flitted once you get weaving around the basket.

5. 1/2" weaver can be from 4' to 6' long. (Usually thinner than the uprights)

Chase weaves with trimming a tapper on the bend to make it look good and has an over under weave.

6. Keep tightening every few rows and keep starting from the bottom to retightening. (For a strong basket)

7. Once at your leveled height of your basket which is 22" finished is what we use. Bend the longer outside ones after socking is worm water in a plastic container top of basket in water to soften the uprights so that will be bent inwards in the inside of the basket. (May take a few hours) You will cut the uprights that are on the inside. (We do not bend on the outside of the baskets with the uprights, it looks ugly and is not needed).

8. Now leveled, put the rim on that will have about a 4" overlap on the inside and outside rims but not in the same place.

9. Green 1" wide by 3/8" thick rims are placed around the top leveled basket and will be held temporary held with clamps. Outside and inside rims are in place which you can start drilling holes landing on the bent uprights if possible. (Going counterclockwise is best way to go).

10. Keep moving and tighten the rawhide with knots on the outside of the basket as you go around the basket.

11. Ending with a tight rim and tying off the rawhide with a knot.

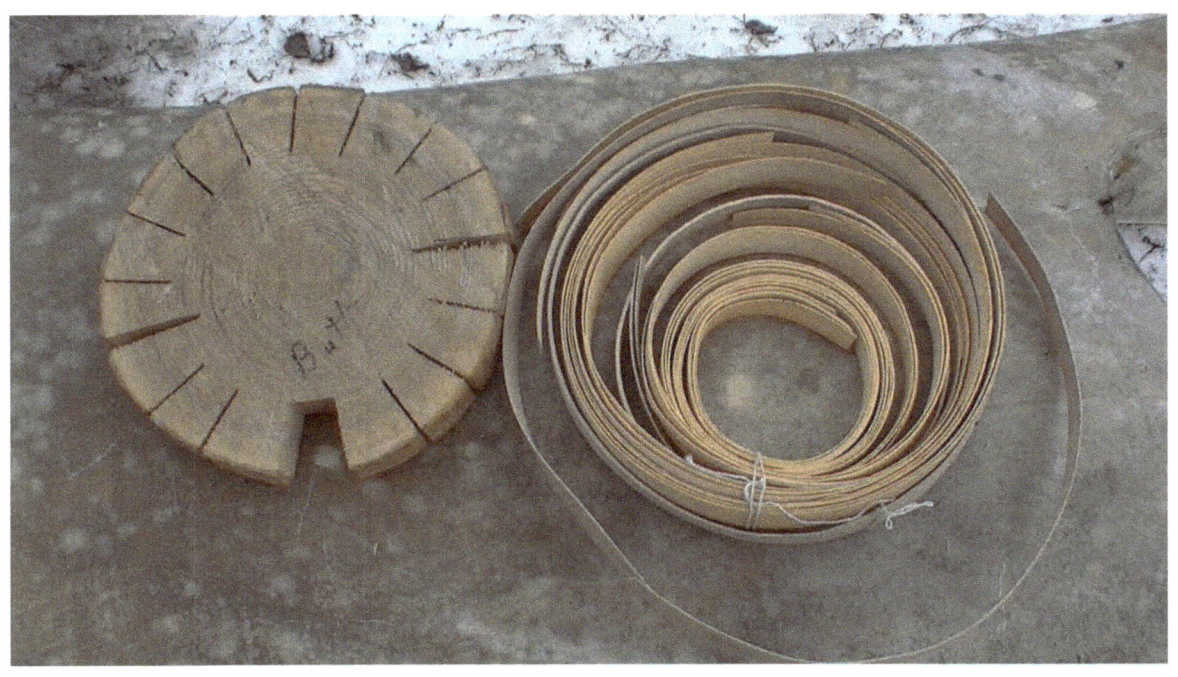

Laundry basket mold

Molds can be made with cedar wood put together so it is tapper and can just slide off once the basket is dried and the rims are ready to be added on. The size of the mold would depend on the size of the basket you want.

The cardboard of the weaving pattern to start the bottom of the laundry basket is 9" wide and 13" long and the sides are 10" high.

Preparing to Weave

Note: Remember the thicker strips should be your uprights and the thinner ones are your weavers.

Tests are done before cutting the strips or pounding the log material you have in front of you. This will help before you start to make a basket. When ash is in small strips, test it for flexibility. Look for strips that do not crack, snap, and/or split. Be sure that your strips are not brittle. Grain strength of the strips is a key. Straight strip fibers and cross weaving makes a basket strong and durable. Testing the flexibility, color, thickness, and width is important to the end product.

You may have many grades and thickness of the weavers and the graded them and how they look once sanded. These entire things make a difference on a basket. The best wood should be sorted and always bent inwards, natural of how it comes off the tree and inwards how a basket is woven. Flatting a start of a basket or whatever can be done with weights being placed where it going to stay flat.

Always make note as to the number of uprights in your basket layout. When you are weaving your over and under, you don't want to end with two weavers under or two inches over after weaving. If for some reason your count is off, you may want to make one of your uprights just a little wider, so you can split it if you need to be able to weave over and under. This will put balance in your design and give strength to your weaving. The key is right amount of uprights. At times you may have to split one for the over and under effect.

Rewetting the outer flat zones of the strips is easy with fresh water. Always use fresh water but remember leaving ash in the same water too long will darken the wood faster. It may take just a spray bottle to mist the ash strips as needed. Clean cold water in a spray bottle works best, but too much water may make the weavers swell up too much and be harder to work with. It will swell the wood, which will not allow strips to move easily. It will leave more cracks once the wood is dry. A wet clean rag might work better at times then if the spray bottles is making it too wet or if you only want to wet a certain area. Practice with watering the ash strips while weaving will make it easier to weave and make a nice basket.

For me, I prefer to do many steps. In this way, the weavings are tight and will not move or loosen. This will also enhance their appearance. When I am designing a basket, I make a pattern on cardboard or typing paper. In this way, I can see the overall pattern before I start to weave.

Bottom weavers should not be too wide because you want to go around the base tightly. If they are too wide, it may not look good, and it will be harder to work with. Start with thinner ones which can take the layer tightening better. Then go a bit wider, especially when making bigger baskets. You are the controller of your basket. Good wood quality that is flexibility works bests. Not all the ash wood is the same; be very picky. Take your time until you master what you are doing, I can never say it enough.

As layers of weaving is completed, you may have to go back many times to retighten the weaving in order to have a great tight looking basket. The larger the basket, the more times you will have to retighten. Once dry, the strips will stay in place and will not move any longer. The more experience you have, the better your baskets will turn out.

As you wait for drying, you may work on other steps. If you have many baskets going at once, your time management will work out better. Keep all the same material you're going to use together so it doesn't' get mixed up. Then you will not have to work hard to find the right upright or weavers that will match the other wood on the basket, unless you want the off colors.

When you know what is needed to make a quality basket, you will see the wood quality and workmanship in baskets that you come across. There is a difference in how baskets are made, so pay attention to what you buy and look for quality. Look at the weaving, but also the thickness of the entire basket weavers and uprights. The uprights should be the thicker ones. It should be all the same wood from the same tree. The strips should not be too thick or too thin, this very important to have a stable balanced basket.

Weaving (Three types)

Note: Try not to land with your overlap joint lined up with other ones. If you do, it may look bad and makes for a weaker basket. Remember that before uprights are moved within the design, it is good to flex each one many times. This will make it easier to put in place without breaking or splintering.

You will want to make your basket with all the same wood at one time. The weaving should all be done within a few days. This will give you a better result. This will allow constancy in weaving and color after drying. It is harder to work on dried basket and will be noticed more if it is different color weavers. As weaving is being done you may have to go back many times to retighten the weaving. This will give you a great tight looking basket. The larger the basket, the more times you will have to retighten. Once dry, the strips are in place and will not move much. Knowing all this will help when making a basket strong and good looking.

There are three main methods to weave baskets that we use: single layer weave, wrap around, and chase. Some people use a double thickness weave around the outside bottom of the basket to last longer and make it stronger. You can put one more layer, even under the basket, for wear and looks. There are so many ways you can start a bottom, you can even invent your own one. There is no right or wrong way if that is the way you want to make them.

*****

Single Layer Weave

The single layer weave is achieved when one piece of weaver goes around and back on into itself with a overlap. It is very easy to do and works well for holding it place one row at a time. It is a great way to make fancy weaving also. You may have more short pieces when you do these baskets, so knowing basket sizes at times helps you use most of your weavers. Splicing can be used on the weaver around joints. Overlap three and stop on the inside so it doesn't show the ends on the outside of the basket or make a bump. This type of weaving is basically doing one layer around at a time is very common. All overlap joints is of three, done on the inside of the basket so it don't show as much.

Many different width sizes make a different look on baskets. Once the basket is made one row a time around, you can retighten and add another strip or a brown twisted rope to match in the small space. Pay close attention to those details that will make your work stand out. Everything you do makes a difference, so take your time and do quality work. Let your imagination run free and make use able art.

Wrap around Weave

This technique uses one weaver. The first weaver is bent over an upright one to hold it in place hooked back about ½ inch. The weaver is woven through the uprights, over and under, over and under until the basket is finished. The overlap weaver is tapered when you reach the rim to level the top. The top section will be covered by the rim, which will hide the tapering. This method can make weaving a basket goes fast, because you can use five feet weavers, and you do not need to connect too many pieces.

Chase Weave

We often use a method of weaving called the chase method. This form of weaving is a little different. We start the pattern with one weaver bent almost in half, weaving two layers at a time. This is a fast and sturdy method, but not so good on fancy baskets.

Using this traditional method of weaving, we bend a weaver almost in half around an upright and bend it to weave back over and just above the same strip, in the opposite direction. These strips should be thin and fine, but not too thick. Start at the bottom and go around the uprights at the bottom over and under clockwise. This will help to keep everything in place. You may want to make a pattern on paper and keep track of how long and how many of the strips and types of strips you will need.

Basket, with two bottoms

First you start flat and start weaving around half of the uprights. Then placing the other half uprights, you weave the other layer of the second bottom. You can just do one bottom all so if you want that without any weaving around which you have really hold it in place, so it doesn't move when weaving around.

You can put the basket on a board and clamp it so that it stays in place. You can make a "lazy Susan" board to work on so everything moves. In this way you can spin the basket without having to move it as you weave around the uprights. In order to keep your basket flat on the bottom and level after you finish each step, we recommend using a round doughnut to hold in the center goes over the bottom to keep it all flat, with a piece of plywood with a heavy weight on it. This will allow it to dry in the correct shape.

    This plywood ring should be cut out in the center, "a doughnut shape", so that the center can be allowed to be convex. Be careful not to allow the weight press down in the center through the hole. Your doughnut should be ¾" thick. I suggest that, after you weave a few layers, let them dry. It is a good idea to go back and tighten every few layers. Keep in mind that once you complete your basket you can't go back to tighten. Keeping a tight weave is the key to stability so that it will not loosen and become weaker. These are just a few of the techniques we can share with you for you to make a great basket. Better strips make great baskets and weaving may take some time to master.

Chase method best for finished basket with the split sides always on the outside.

Bottom

    At the start of making a basket, it is a good idea to use a weight to flatten your center bottom before weaving your uprights. You need to know how to start and lock the bottom in place, so it doesn't move once you start to weave. If the start of the weaving is unstable or uneven it will be hard to move the weavers back into place. Rubber bans can be helpful holding the uprights in place while weaving around.

    Pushpins can be used to hold your ash upright strips to the bottom of your wooden mold but not threw the wood just do it in between the strips. Small screws can be used to attach strips to the mold for larger baskets, such as pack baskets. Clamps or weights can also be used just as long the strips stay put while you start going around with a good weaver.

    At the bottom outside of basket, you may add double weavers because that's where it takes a beating. Pack basket really need that extra strength. When bottoms need to be sturdy, you can sometimes use extra bottom weavers instead of wood runners. Using the runners do help keep the basket off the ground in ice. Thick strips help, but you really need those ¾" runners.

Remember the key is when making the bottom of the basket; you want to keep it flat. You might use bricks on the bottom ring. This will help keep the bottom of the basket flat and it will stay flat as it dries. When the center bump goes inwards overnight, it will give a good shape to the basket. You may give it more time to completely dry.

Using pattern on card boards or thin plywood and color the different squares where the bottom ash strips will lay and where you start makes it easier until you know it by heart. Making the bottom of basket hold all the wood strips together can be thicker ash strips or flat for now uprights and hold in place, at times you wish you had another hand push pin can be used. Use only the fine flexible weavers to start with on round baskets and then bigger ones or larger ones. Not all ash trees have quality wood. As you are using the strips and if you find a bad one doesn't use it. That is where testing in your hands to find the best piece of ash and even keep testing with your hands and weak spot don't use.

A cardboard cutout for the start of a bottom basket can help line everything up with your strip on top of the square placement. Colored squares or rectangles marked, and it's the best for pack basket which will fit perfect on the bottom or other square or rectangles. This is important because it ready for the correct weave placement.

Finishing Top Weave

Sometimes, to make it work just right, you must split an upright that split upright may be thicker where it will be split and thinner on the other side to make it look good. Make sure you know which one you want to split so it can be weighted and split on one side to make it look even. This split is for the over and under. For the most strength, this is best, but for a different look there are other ways of weaving which make it look good. Once the basket is finished and well dried, but still is loose, you will want to tighten it a bit more. You can retighten the weavers or add items like sweet grass or other things if you want to make it look and feel tighter.

Bending Around the Rim

Note: Be careful it doesn't split on you. Use good bending ash rims, green rims if you are to nail or rawhide. Predrill is a must, as you go counterclockwise, clamping as you go around leaving clamps in place until dry. **The finished rim uprights should be just a bit higher than the top edge (1/16"). Be careful to tapper the ends of the inside and outside rims with a knife and/or hacksaw when almost at the end of the rims. You can make it ahead of time on the table saw, the tapper once you know the size. Make a good long tapper depending on the size of the basket. Bend over the alternate one toward the inside and evenly cut the next one. With the uprights bent inwards on the basket, they should not be seen. This is done so nothing will catch on the strips when moving them in and out. The bend strips should be woven two or three layers deep down the weavers which can be covered at the end if they are done right. Last rim overlaps and inside overlap of both end pieces, which should be about 4 inches also the inside overlap rims on small baskets and more on larger ones.**

~ 179 ~

~ 180 ~

Rims

Rims need to be constructed from a good strong and thicker piece of wood. 1/16" to ¼" to 3/8" or more as the basket is bigger. It should be in proportion to the size of the basket for strength. Rims go around the inside and outside of the top of the basket. Use clamps to hold them together as you complete the edge and for a while afterward to ensure that it stays in place. The inside and outside joint overlap should not be at the same place for looks and strength. We like to the rims outside the handles, one on one side and on the other side of the basket with a notch on the inside for more strength. A rim holds everything together and is the key part of a basket that makes it sturdy. When cutting and sizing your strips, put the thicker ones for rims aside for this purpose.

NAILS NOTE: You may want to pre-drill holes in the centers of the alternate uprights to prevent splitting (the uprights bent inwards of the basket and need to be predrilled for rawhide). Uprights that would be bending on outside are cut flush.

One way to complete the rim is to use nails. The nails are put in the upright's wider strips that are bent back inwards in green ash (dry rims may crack if you don't predrill). You want that nail heads to be on the outside of the basket and on the inner folded upright for best grip, have some on all uprights. Use wax or water on the nail to help the nail slide in the predrilled hole. The hole should be smaller than the nail diameter so it will not split. The bent nails on the basket rim should always be bent over the grain or 90 degrees for the holding power.
(Picture of overlaps, bent ones, cut ones, nail rig, nail placement)

Clamping as you go around is very important to hold where you're nailing only. Keep moving around with clamps as you nail around keep adding clamps. Make sure it is very tight and use plenty of good clamps, so nothing moves. Leave the clamps on a few days on the rim or until dry. You may even have to go around and re nail at times. The reasons that the nails are inwards is it would catch on everything it the nails were on the outside. But after time, it catches stuff on the inside; you may have to re pound the nails in time. Rawhide is a onetime rim holder that we think is the best.

Taper the last overlap of the rim of both ends pieces, which should be about 4 inches, and clamp until it is dry all around even once done for a few days. You may want to put 2 or 3 nails there at the end of the overlap and keep the clamps if using nails. Be careful with too many nails because it will want to split on you. You don't want a big bump, so plan the connection well ahead with the measurement.

HANDLE

A table saw and or a draw shaver work well for shaping the handles. Most handles are made on a form and dried before being used. A good handle mold works well to dry the handle in shape. You can bend free style if you want. You can use plain handles half round or a designed handle. Things depend on your taste and what you want. It's your basket drill the handles are a must do for no split outs on the wood handles.

Keep the wooden handle in a dry dark place until needed to keep the natural color. What that does is keep the wood whiter or bright and fresh looking, and sand only before using the handle.

Green handles can be used, but it may make your basket a bit shaky once dry and crooked. Handles can be made with just ash strips or many year growths to the thickness you want and made into the shape you want. The handle can have two nails on the outside wooden part over the rims. And. The handles could also be made with deer or moose anthers and tied on with rawhide attached to the rims. Feel free to try all kinds of free natural things around you.

A notch on the inside of the handle helps carry heavy loads which locked it all together and make for a strong basket that looks good. The size of the notches depends on the size of the inside of the rim. The handle should be quite dry when making the notches. The handle should only notch before connecting it to the rims so you know the right size to cut and remove the notch. This is mostly for the carrying weight the basket might have. Picture here Handle also should go down on the inside a few weavers.

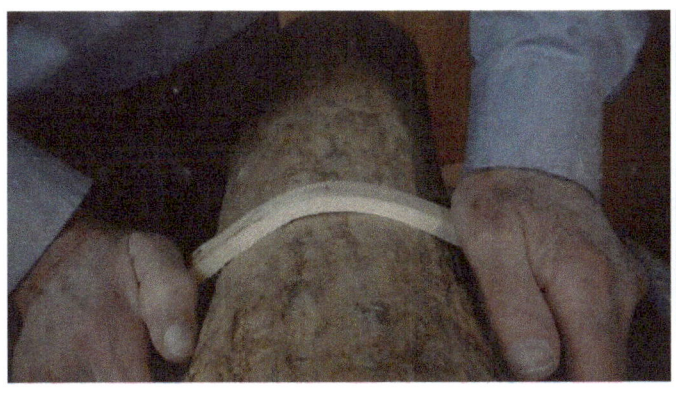 

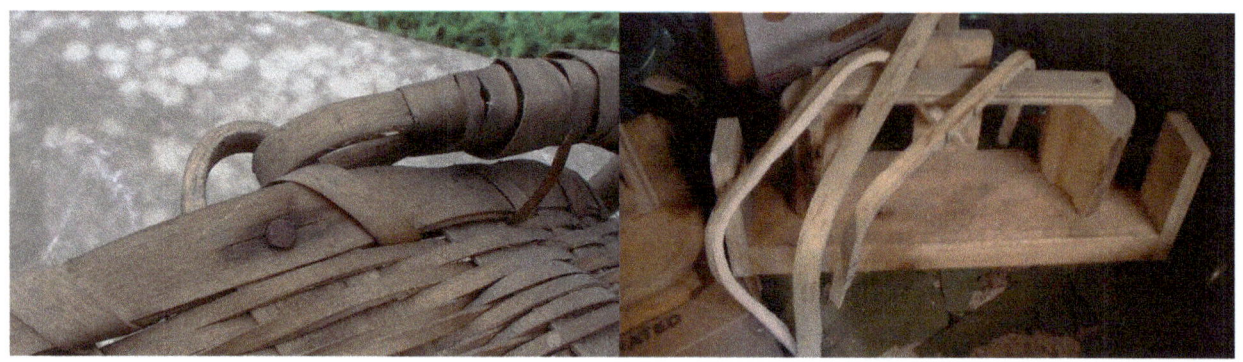

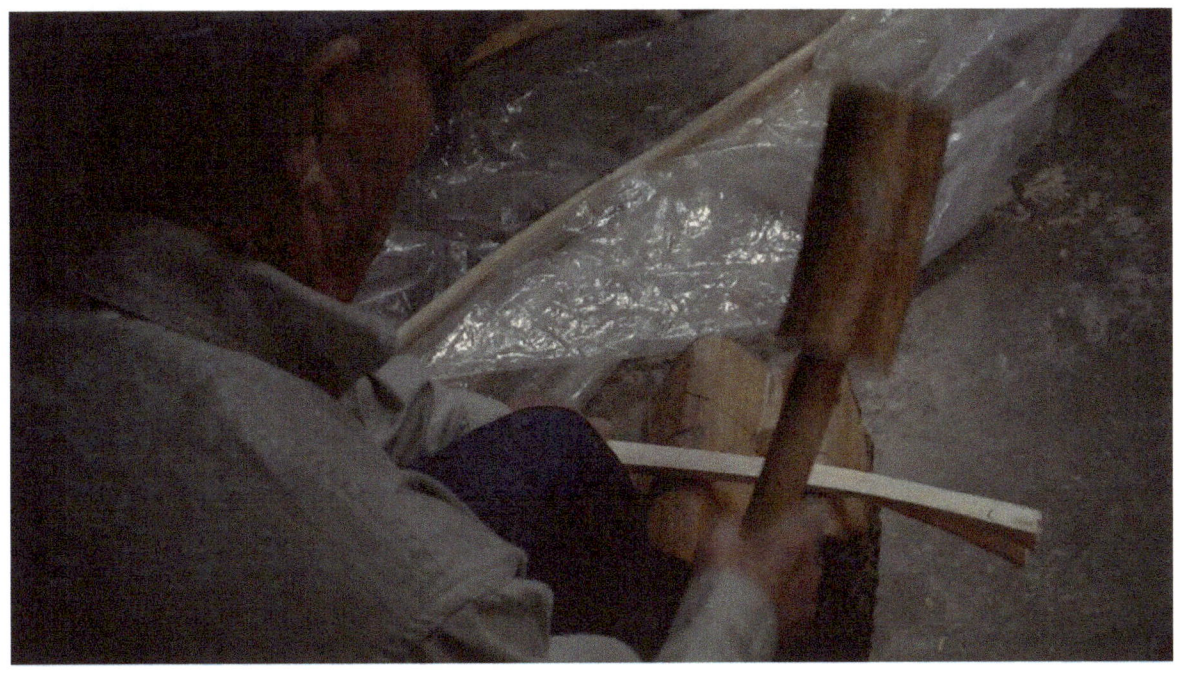

Nails on the Handle

When nailing ash basket rims and handles to each other, short long pointy nails are used. If you can get them, shoe nails are best. There are many sizes and lengths of flexable, thin, pointy points. Your basket size will determine the nail size. You don't want a big nail on a small basket. These nails are made for the fine point to bend when hit into metal.

At some places next to the handle you may want to place two nails to make sure it holds good and tight; you always need to do this. You should pre-drill the holes. These nails should not go through the wood, so they do not need to be bent. The notch will vary with the type of handle and the thickness. Some judgment from your part will be needed.

Wrapping

We don't like using nails any longer then we need it when tying basket rims unless someone requests it. We use small pre-stretched rawhide. We put a knot as we go around, so it doesn't move. We prefer no metal in our basket. Yes, using ash strips with rawhide for the looks. This is best and works the best for us for many reasons, strong hold, and fast and looks different and great. This lasts a long time. We also use ash wrapping on some fancy baskets.

Cover

NOTE: Cover your work well to stop things from falling into the basket, like rain, and junk when out in the bush.

There are many basket sizes, shapes, and styles that you can create.

Start Weaving the first bottom of basket, then there is a second inside bottom. 1 is the very bottom of basket. Lay your bottom which also will be come your upright. If you want a stronger basket weave both bottom.

1-4   8   2

First Bottom

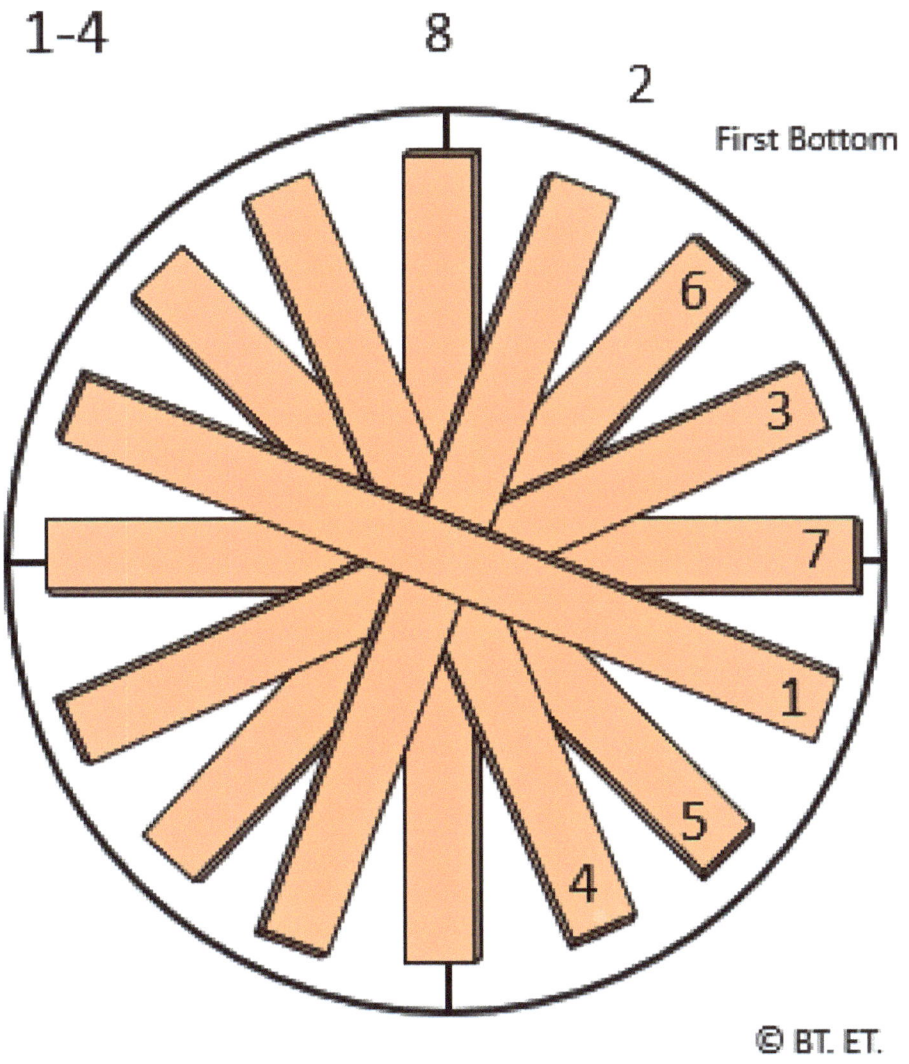

© BT. ET.

First Bottom

Best way of doing this is one layer at a time with a over lap a few of the bottom ones. Always over under, over under to hold every thing together with a weaver.

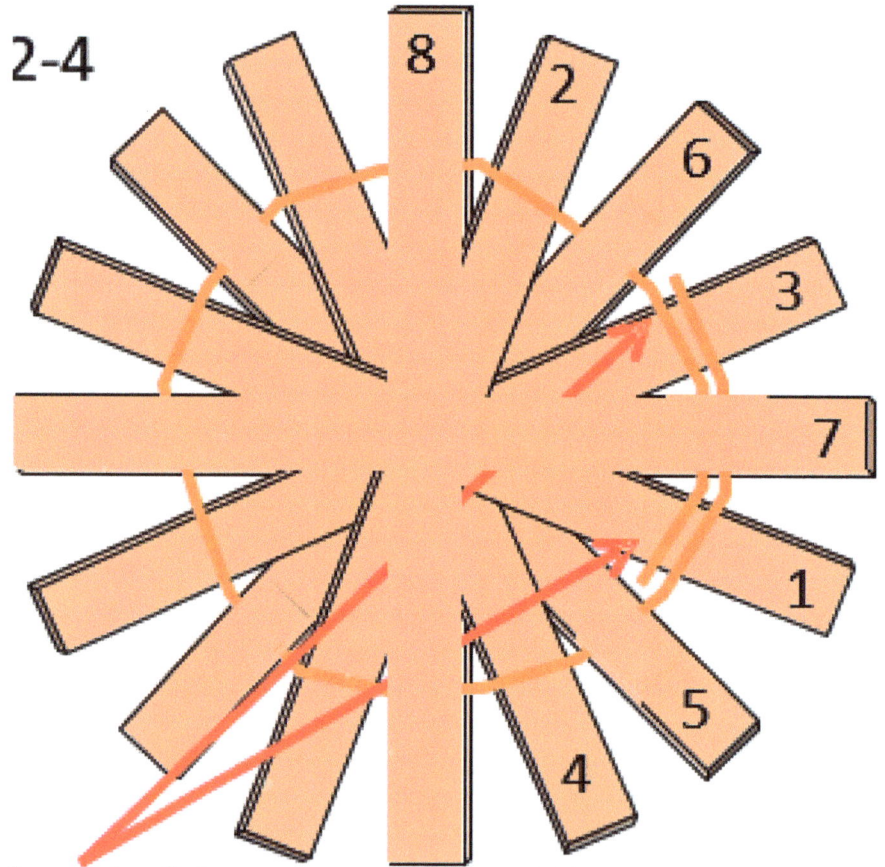

The ends of the weaver ends should be hidden and almost as long as bottom strip it's under.

© BT. ET.

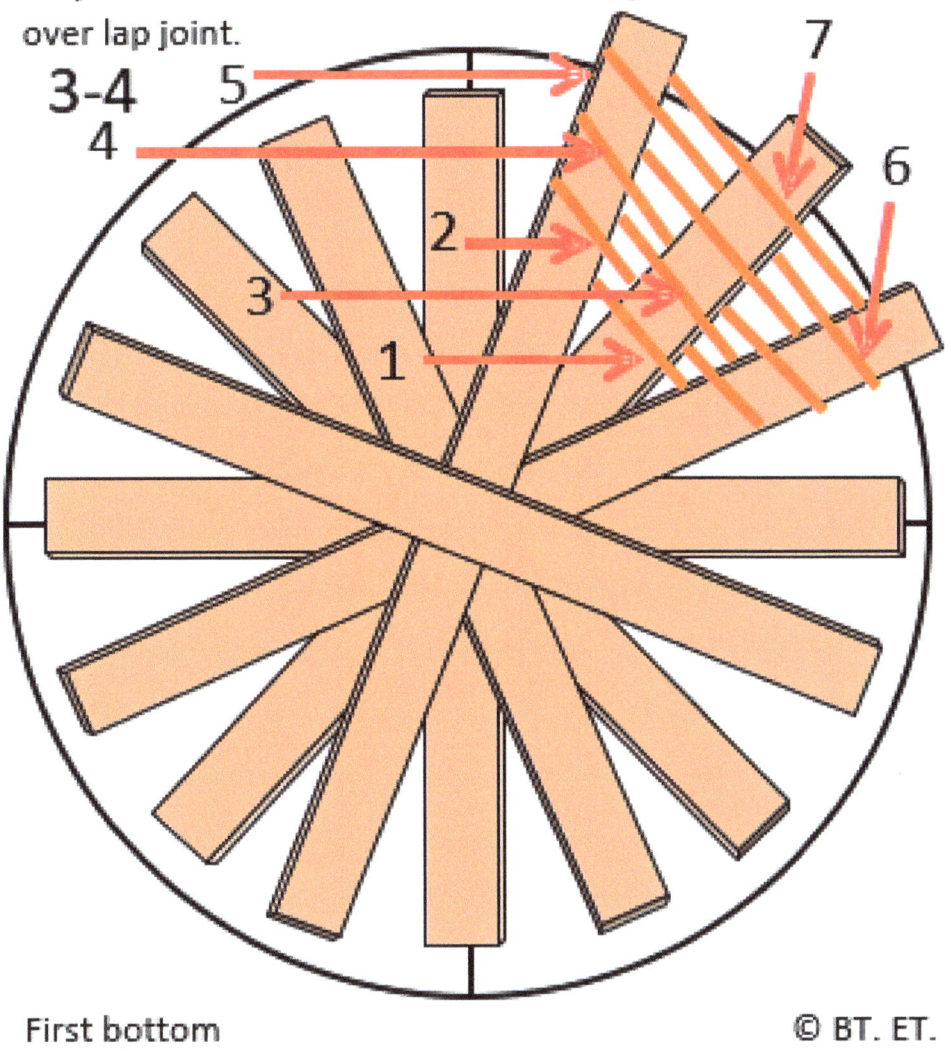

Start Weaving the first bottom of basket, then there is a second inside bottom. Go around with weaver about 7 times around depending on your width of your weaving strips. You can weave around one strip at a time with a over lap joint.

First bottom   © BT. ET.

Now weaving the 2nd bottom of basket, which is the inside of the basket. Lay down the next 8 bottom strips on top of 1st bottom strips. And keep on weaving until the bottom is done. Then push the uprights easily in place which can be held with rubber bans on the mold. Then you can start weaving the side of the basket, over and under one row a time if that the weave you want to use.

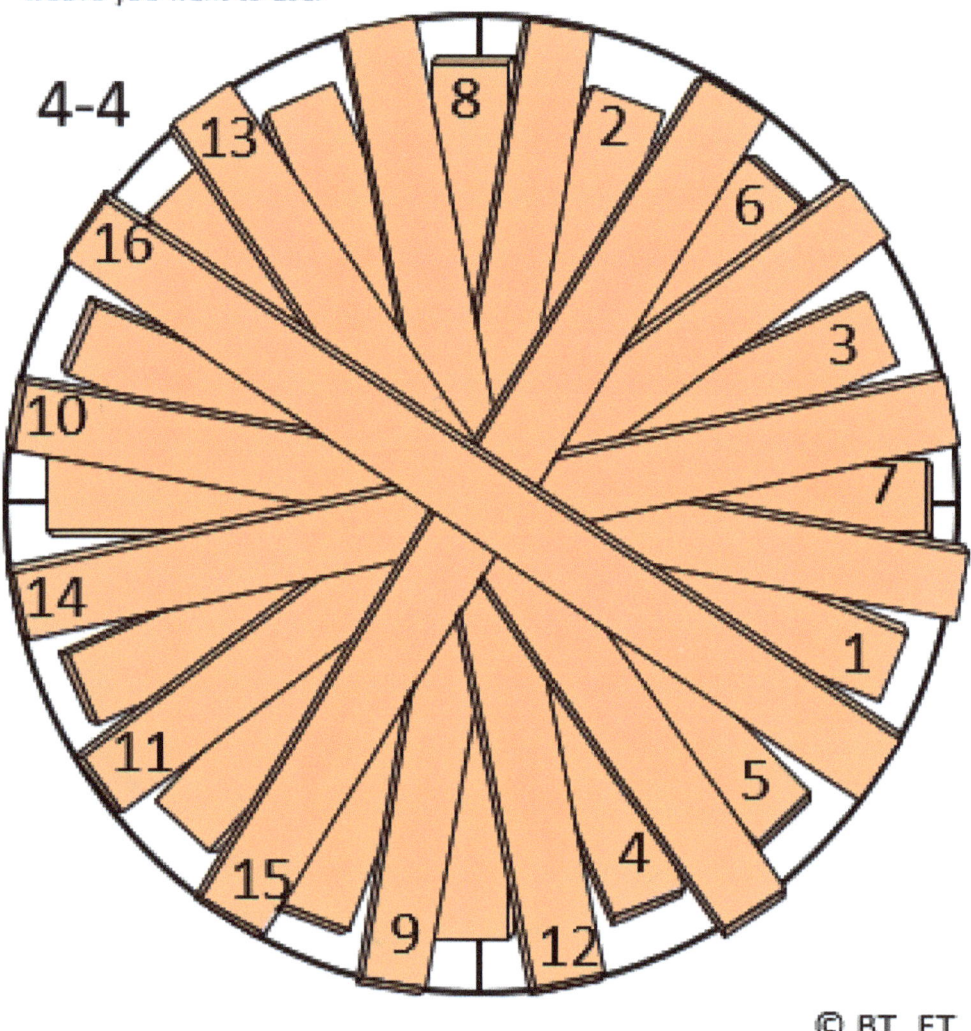

4-4

© BT. ET.

Key to flat round bottom baskets

Wood doughnut rings that are placed inside of the bottom of the basket with weight on the rings on a hard flat surface is key to a flat basket.

Bricks or metal weight.

You may have to keep the weight in the basket a few days or more or until basket is dry. Use before the rim is done and once the basket is done.

Make sure that the ring fits the basket you are making. You need different ring sizes for different baskets. This ring lets the bottom strips come up inside the ring.

The ring can be ¾" thick, 1 or more depending how big the basket is.

Notes: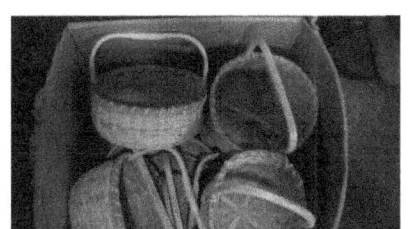

• CHAPTER 9 •

MAKING OF BASKETS

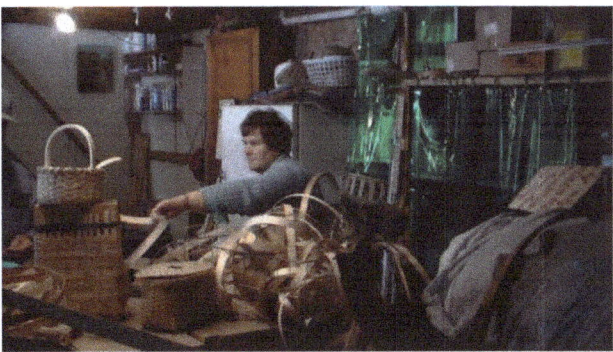

Laundry basket 1-5

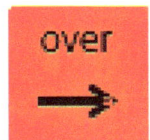 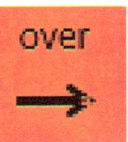

The four red corner are on the bottom of the basket.

9-1" x 13-1" upright spaced out evenly in a weaved pattern.

© BT. ET.

| 1 | 2 | 3 | 4 | 5 | 6 | 7-9 |

↓ ↓ ↓ ↓ ↓ ↓ ↓

Under and over, under and over, so on.

1 Over and under ash strip for bottom of laundry basket. Keep the spaces as even as possible.

2 Bottom of basket, outside of the tree. Nine inches by thirteen inches bottom.

3 The four corners are on the bottom of the basket.

4 One inch wide or close to one inch, for uprights is used.

5 Six feet long or shorter is needed for bottom bent up to upright is needed for this pack basket.

6 Weaver are about one inch wide and thinner.   **2-5**

7 Weavers are one row long at a time. and the over lap can be three times and end on the inside of basket.

8 Over and under, over under weave is very strong. Keep tighten every three rows, for strength.

9-13 Flex uprights many times easy.   © BT. ET.

Laundry basket   3-5

Start here, use the single row weave, over under and so on. 9 rows high, all 1" wide uprights and weavers.

Screw on a 9"x13"x3/4" board to hold down the uprights in place on the bottom of the mold in the empty spaces.

Strong 3 over lapping weaving joint.   © BT. ET.

Laundry basket 4-5
Bended ash Handle on both side or rope.

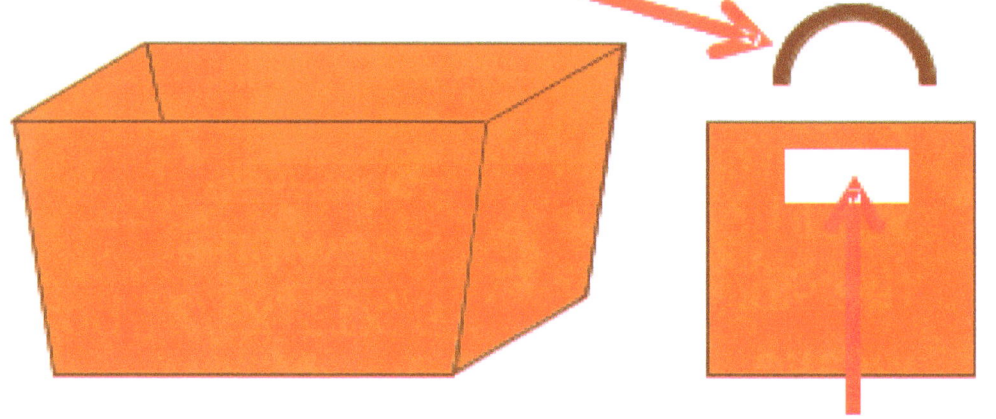

Open Handle is best.

Strong 3 over lapping weaving joint is best and very strong.

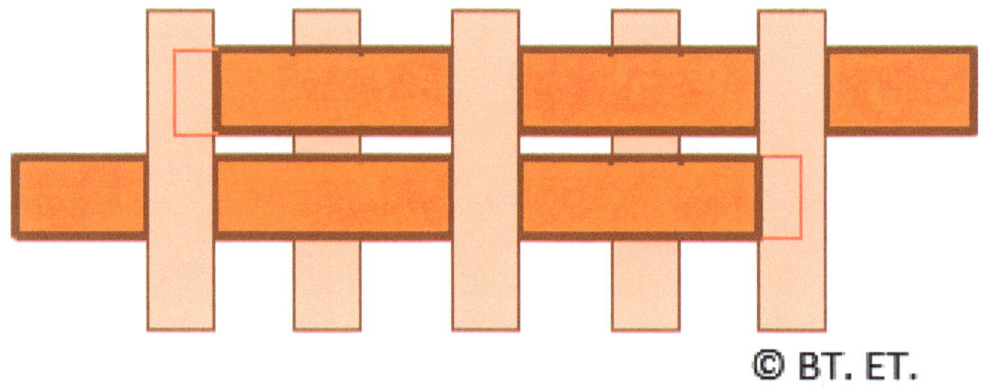

© BT. ET.

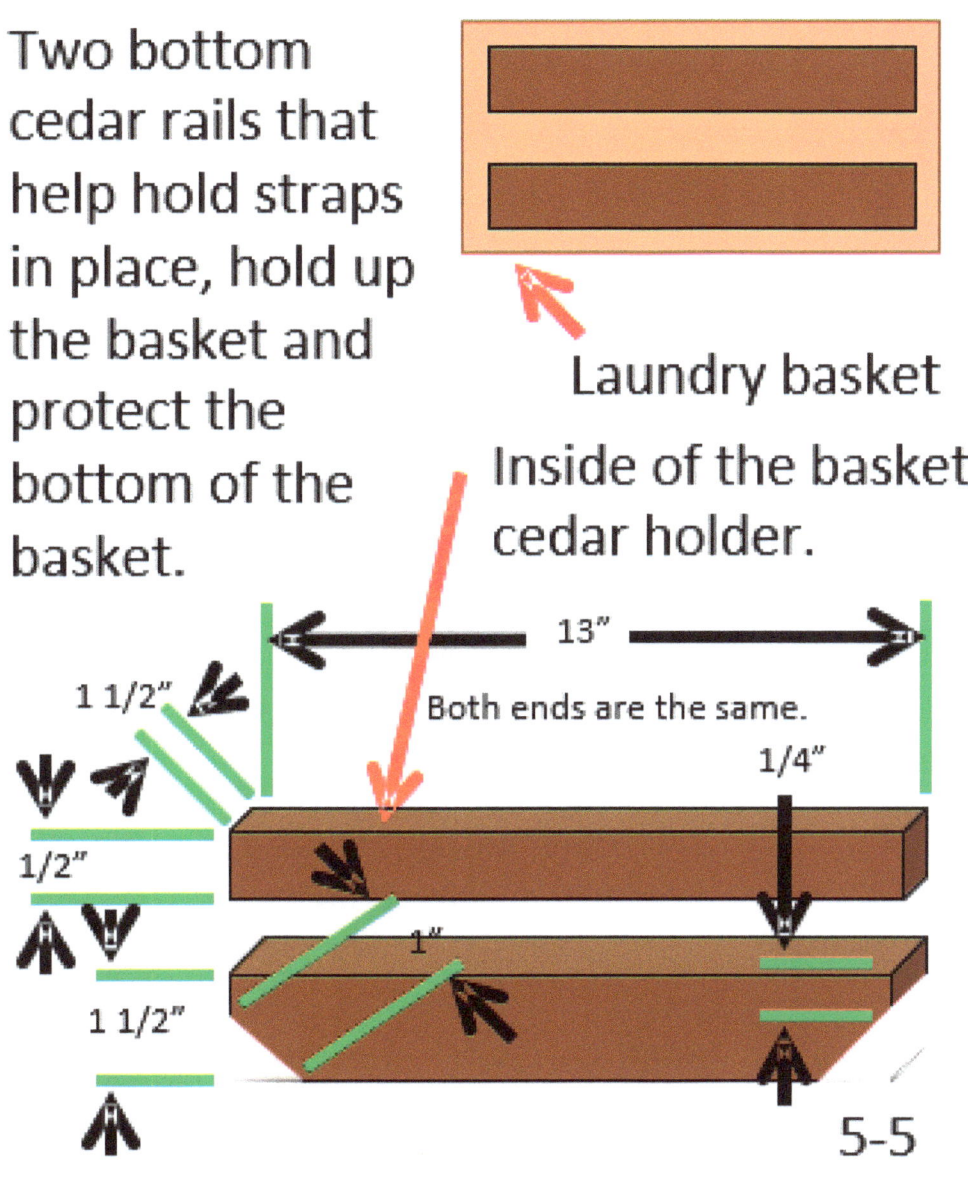

Pack basket 1-9

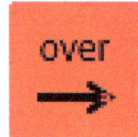 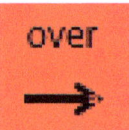

The four red corner are on the bottom of the basket.

7-1" x 9-1" upright spaced out evenly in a weaved pattern.

© BT. ET.

1　2　3　4　5　6　7
↓　↓　↓　↓　↓　↓　↓
Under and over, under and over, so on.

1 Over and under ash strip for bottom of pack basket. Keep the spaces as even as possible.

2 Bottom of basket, outside of the tree. Seven inches by nine inches bottom.

3 The four corners are on the bottom of the basket.

4 One inch wide or close to one inch, for uprights is used.

5 Six feet long is needed for bottom bent up to upright is needed for this pack basket.

6 Weaver are about half inch wide and thinner.   2-9

7 Weavers can be 4 feet long or longer, and the over lap can be three times and end on the inside of basket.

8 Over and under, over under weave is very strong. Keep tighten every three rows, for strength.

9 Flex many times easy, do not bent just once.© BT. ET.

Back of pack basket for your back.

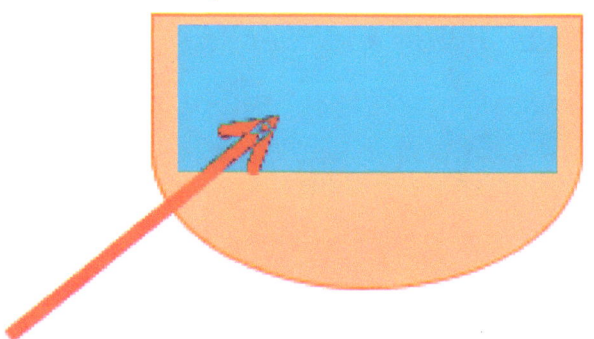

Screw on a board to hold down the uprights on the bottom of the mold in the empty spaces. 7"x 9"x ¾" board .

3-9

© BT. ET.

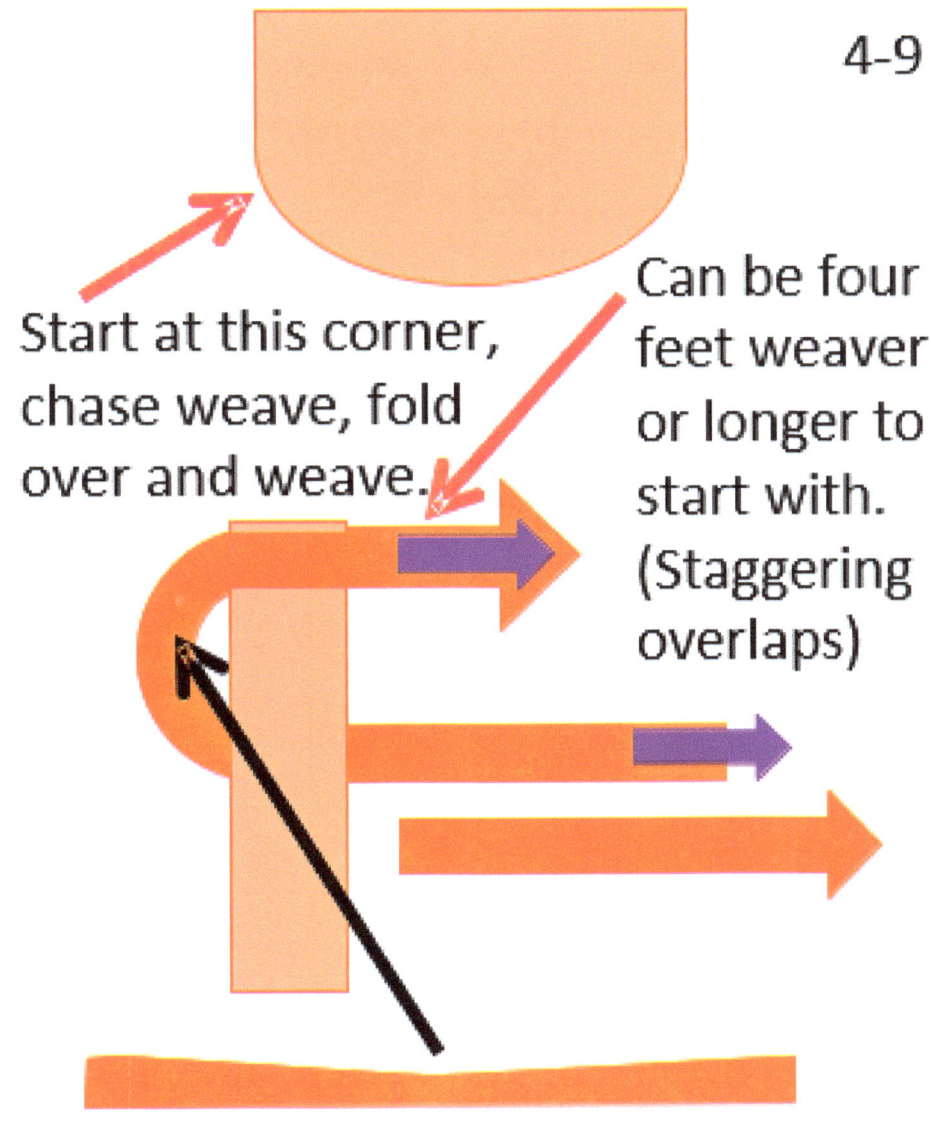

4-9

Start at this corner, chase weave, fold over and weave.

Can be four feet weaver or longer to start with. (Staggering overlaps)

Tapper where you start.

© BT. ET.

Pack basket   5-9

Strong 3 over lapping weave once you have to add another weaver, over lapping joint should always be stronger joints on the basket. (Do not put joints at the same places).

Row 2, 3, etc.

1   2   3

Row 1.

© BT. ET.

Pack basket 6-9

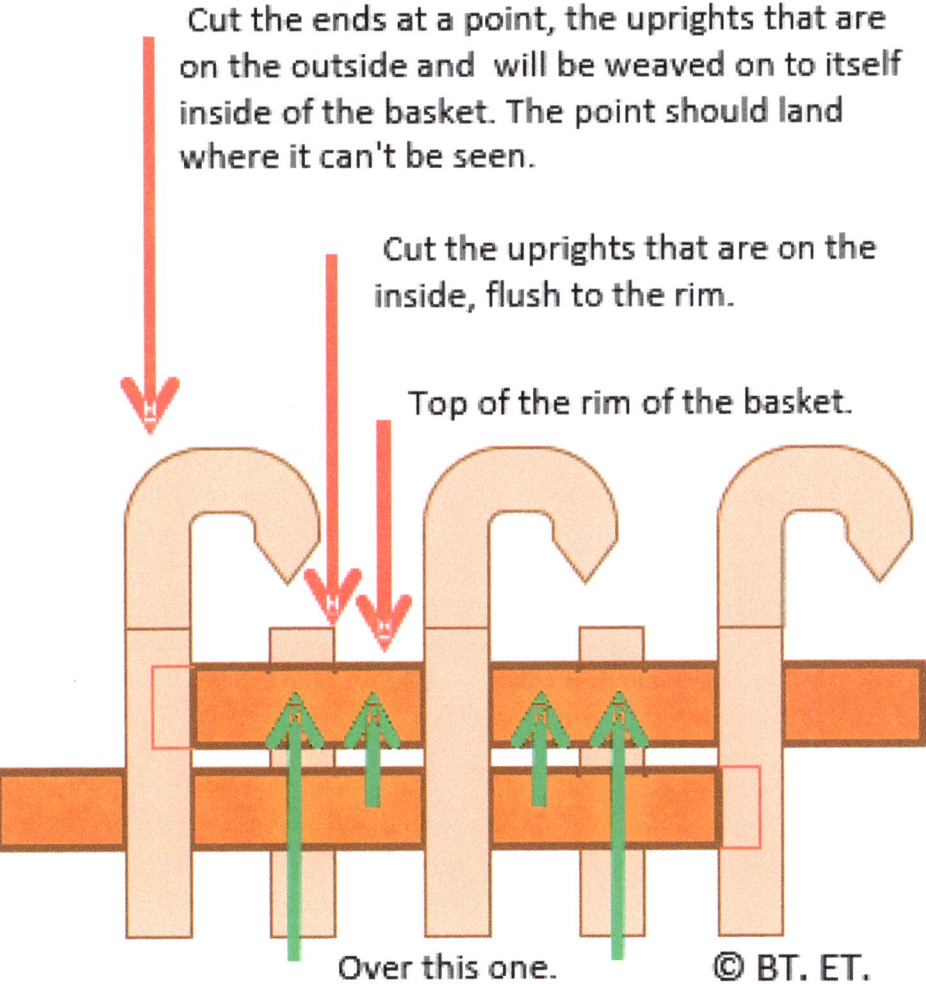

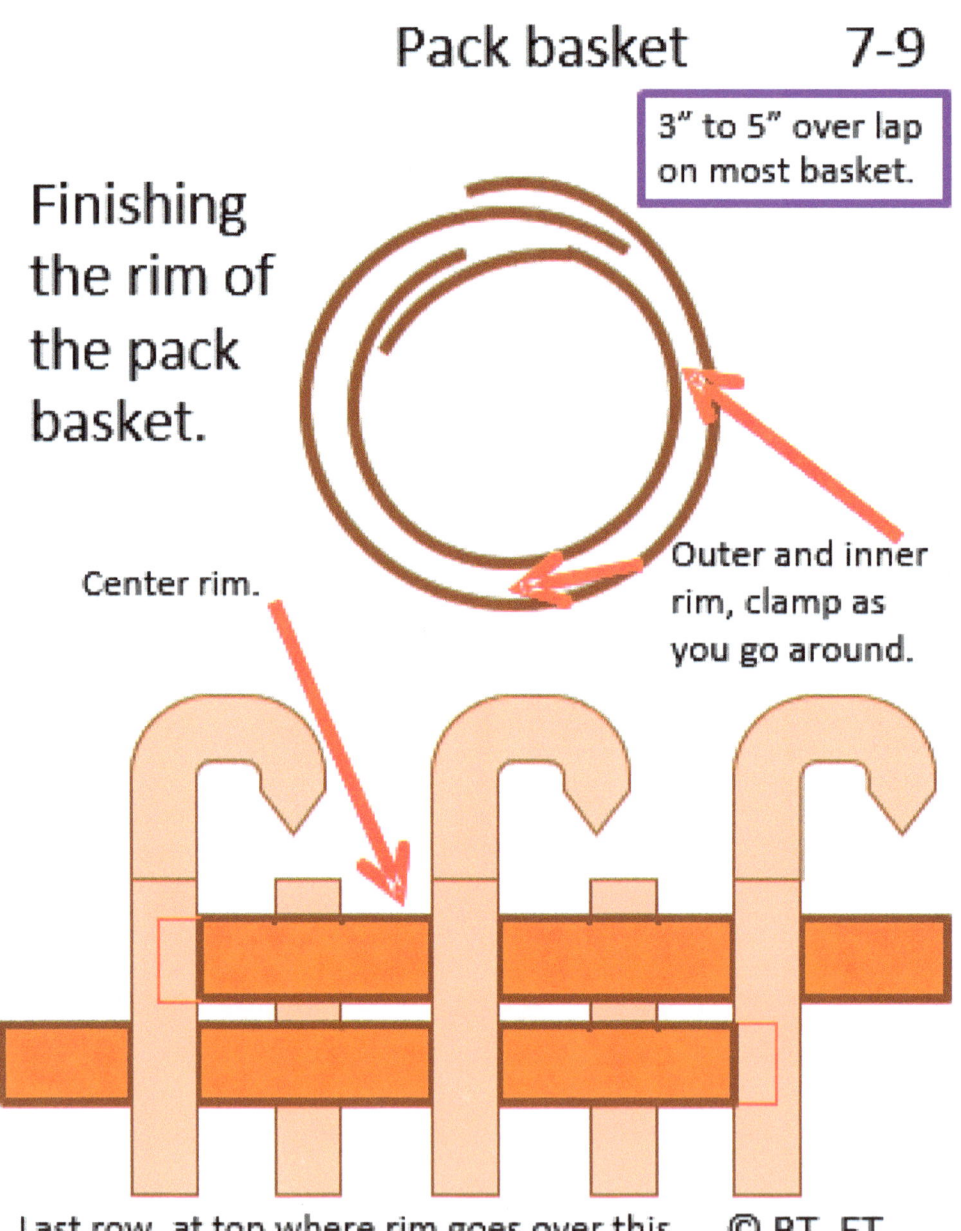

Pack basket
Rims

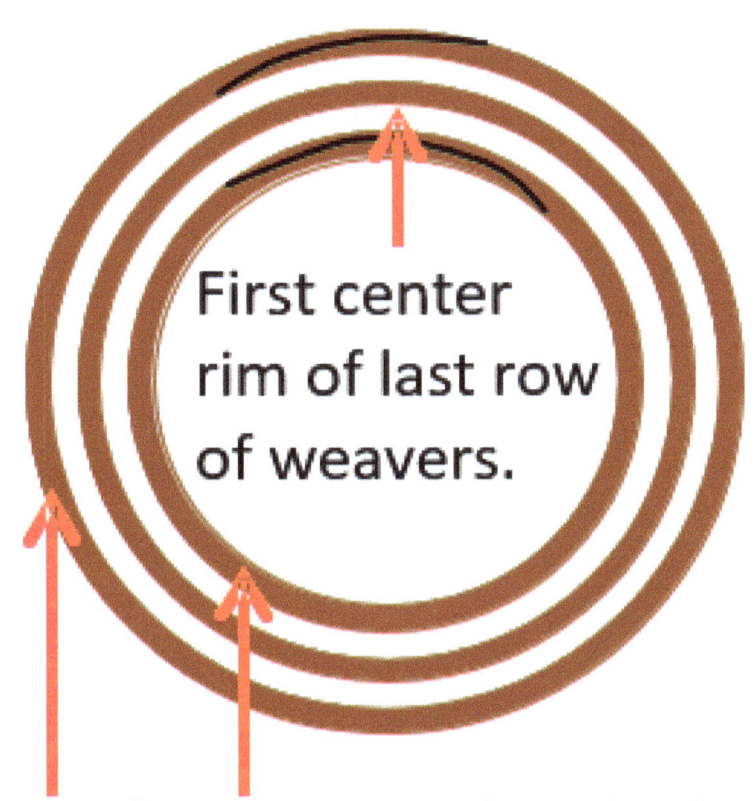

First center rim of last row of weavers.

Outer & inner over lap rim is placed on at same time.

© BT. ET.

Two bottom cedar rails that help hold straps in place, hold up the basket and protect the bottom of the basket.

Basket

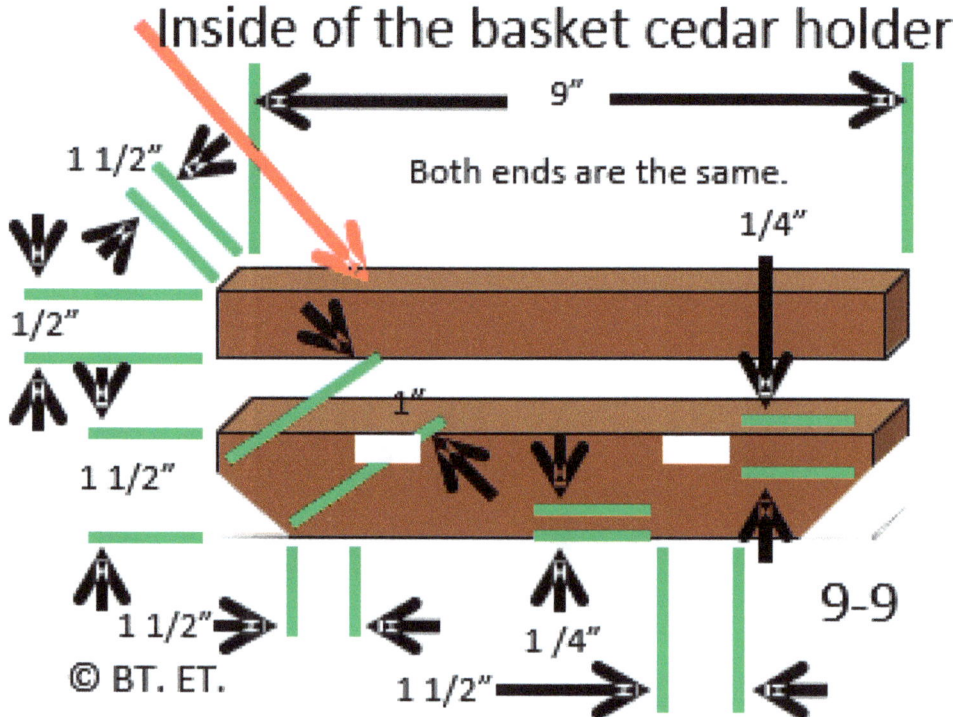

Inside of the basket cedar holder.

Both ends are the same.

9-9

© BT. ET.

• CHAPTER 10 •

CARE OF BASKETS

Plain baskets show the wood color and pattern. Sometimes the basket has more value if you leave it natural. There are many basket collectors, but the economy does make the price goes up and down. If you keep raw ash wood, keep in mind that will darken to a dark brown color with time. Hot linseed oil can be used with a clean cotton rag to season the wood and make it last longer. Just rub it on the basket. Some people use bear grease, with can also help the wood last.

It is important to decide if you want to varnish the end product or keep the natural wood. Varnish can help the basket if it is well made. Also consider, varnished baskets look good at first, but an outdoor basket will not dry as well and crack. Varnish can be applied, and two coats are best. Paint is used sometimes, but I do not recommend it, unless it is a special wood paint but even then it loses value. To prep for varnishing or painting, lightly sand. Make sure the basket is dry before applying the first coat. When dry, put on second coat to complete the seal.

Old baskets are brittle. When you come across old baskets in a friend's home or in a shop, are very careful handling them. They may be worth a lot of money, depending on the maker. Look to see if they are signed, and if the maker is well known or famous. Most basket makers leave their mark somewhere on the basket. How they finish them for example can give information about the maker. There were many basket makers in the old days. There was a great need for them especially in agricultural area. The need is not as high today, but there will always be a need for ones with high skills and beautiful baskets.

FIXING

An older basket can be repaired if it is still in good shape and the damage is not too bad. You can eliminate what is spoiled. You can save old worn baskets, and sometimes use parts of the old one to repair other. Saving older or no good baskets also for just to repair others is a good idea. You may have to soak the older repair strips in water to reuse them. You can use new strips, also, but you will want similar colors. It works well to use whatever matches best.

When repairing a broken upright or weaver strip, it is important that your new repair strip is much longer than where the break has occurred. You can repair the break by weaving an ash strip on both sides of the broken strip and tuck the ends so they will not show. This new strip should take up the slack and help strengthen the broken strip. The broken strip need not be removed. It is important to use the same width as the broken strip.

Pre-drill any holes in a repair strip after the nail or rivet has been removed, once the new strip is in place. In this way, when the new nail or rivet is put in place, the new strip won't split. Green wood will not split as easily, but it is still a good idea to pre-drill the new strip once it is in place.

We quite often use cut rawhide strips and predrilled holes as we clamp and go around the rim when ready to tie that spot. Drill all holes around the rim or whatever could move. Here again, it is important to note that when you use rawhide or black spruce root to attach the rim, start your weave ninety degrees from where your handle will be attached. In this way the handle placement will not interfere with the start/finish site of the rim or weaving.

Your rim will look much better if you use these techniques; work rims completely around, keep it tight. Take your time. Different rims and handles may need extra care to make it all work out. There will always be a bit of give even when all it tight. You want this because handles are very important when they carry a lot of weight. They must be strong and be able to handle weight. Potato baskets are a good example of baskets that can be an overload.

• CHAPTER 11 •

Continuing Knowledge

In Northern Maine, we do things a bit differently because our way of life is sometimes hard. This area was a place where your life may depend on this art form for survival. People have changed through the times. Growing pains are part of life, I guess. I hope people realize tradition is part of our life and that we need keep it for future generations.

Baskets were made for survival. They also were formed into odd shapes and sizes that could be constructed with Brown Ash. An expression of your dreams can be created and live on, in your work. When you are a basket maker, you can put your own touch on whatever you make or whatever fills your needs. Let this art form become a passion in your life.

If you start making baskets, and are making a good product, it will be something very special. You can advertise, and soon people will come knocking at your door. If you dedicate yourself to making truly great baskets, collectors and museums will come calling. And will pay a very good price for your creations. When you reach this level, you may be asked to demonstrate, do a talk, or a show-and-tell. If you get really good, you may be asked to teach at schools and demonstrate at fairs or sportsman shows. A person could start their own business by selling pounded ash strips and all types and sizes of rawhide. Not many people are doing this. It could be the beginning of a new business enterprise for you.

I speak about basket making all the time, even when I'm at a sportsman show or demonstrating basket and snowshoe making. I often talk to people who want to know information about basket making. When you show people, especially kids, the skills involved with this craft, their eyes widen as they listen to the tasks involved. They really like to know more and try tasks such as pounding a log when they can get a chance. I like telling what I have learned over the years and making sure, if someone makes a basket, it will be a good job. I want people to learn as much as they can about ash baskets because it is a good art form to know and to be proud of.

We are losing our heritage and traditions really fast when it comes to the old ways. Just because we have books on how to make baskets does not mean it will be passed down to the next generations or even be kept alive. We have to do a lot more to help keep this dying art ongoing. The wood furnishes us with the materials to continue with our skills. The human will provide the knowledge our past elder to our now present day utilized. The ultimate feeling to keep this information from extinction for future is the ambition. The tradition will live in our hearts, minds, words, and handy work. Quality of the artisan work will always be in demand. Satisfaction with our heritage and our culture doesn't have to be in the museum only. Our creations are often meant to be in our hands and used.

I think it would be good to teach these art skills in schools, especially the younger ones. I know, for me, it's very important to keep our past knowledge. I have worked hard to keep basket and snowshoe making around, in our family and into the community and world. Hopefully this book can help be a guide to know what we have done to develop this skill and give you some insights into the basket making craft.

Just let your imagination run wild and make a magnificent usable art. Research all the different types and styles of traditional baskets and how they are made. Baskets have been made and past on for so many years all over the world all types, this so much of a tradition. The family creating together is a way of making memories. Try to have everyone do the process so it will be a life-long process that can be passed down. Do your own style, but keep within the old traditions. This is a good way to go!

These ideals are my main reasons for writing this book.

Notes:

CHAPTER 12 •

Pictures

Conclusion

    I want more people around the world to learn how to make traditional baskets, and this sharing of information is a great part of my goal. I would like to have a place where people could come together and talk about making baskets. I know they communicate on the internet; I would like to have a chartroom to talk about baskets and making them. I enjoy talking with people who want to know more about making baskets. It is difficult to go into too much detail unless they really want to make them. The kids I meet encourage me. I really like talking with; them because they are the next generation to share the pass the knowledge. They may just want to learn about baskets and using the traditional baskets, or they may take up basket making.

    It seems like there is now a small movement to learn and bring the art of traditional basket making alive. The usage is growing fast also, but many people are only willing to pay just so much for a basket unless you have a great basket and billed up your name. I predict that someday, people will be willing to pay more, for a high-quality traditional basket. I have been doing all kinds of things to bring baskets to life in my own ways. I try to attend all kinds of activities and events to demonstrate and share my knowledge of baskets. I have stored **my**

information on a DVD and in this book. I use the internet to reach out to more people. I bring my basket wherever I go. Many people have come up to me and talked about my baskets. It is what I like to do and life's a great privilege to meet so many people.

Once you see how baskets are made and use them, your appreciation will be greater. I have big dreams for traditional basket making. I do see this knowledge extending beyond the state of Maine, to other states, and other countries including Canada. How can I tell it to the world? I feel that I need to get out there more and let people know about baskets in the best way I can, by sharing our knowledge. I do see some changes, which are good, but there could be so much more.

978-0-9910069-0-8   Hard cover Leaving Tracks: A Maine Tradition May, 2014
978-0-9910069-9-1   Soft cover Leaving Tracks: A Maine Tradition

978-0-9910069-2-2   Nature and Maine Hunter Communicate
978-0-9910069-3-9   Nature and Maine Hunter Communicate / EPUB

978-0-9910069-4-6   The Great Depression
978-0-9910069-5-3   The Great Depression / EPUB

978-0-9910069-7-7   BB hard   Brown Ash Baskets: A North American Tradition
978-0-9910069-1-5   BB Soft   Brown Ash Baskets: A North American Tradition
978-1-64516-150-9   BB EPUB   Brown Ash Baskets: A North American Tradition
DVD Movie-----------------------------Brown Ash Baskets: A North American Tradition

978-0-9910069-8-4   SS hard   Brown Ash Snowshoes: A North American Tradition
978-1-64516-149-3   SS EPUB   Brown Ash Snowshoes: A North American Tradition
978-0-9910069-6-0   SS soft   Brown Ash Snowshoes: A North American Tradition
DVD Movie-----------------------------Brown Ash Snowshoes: A North American Tradition

Brian J. Theriault

Hudson Bay – red and black wool blanket jacket-trade value: 3 ½ beavers

Traditional brown ash basket and snowshoes with a double bit axe on the St John river.

www.ingramcontent.com/pod-product-compliance
Lightning Source LLC
Chambersburg PA
CBHW061141010526
44118CB00026B/2835